The History of Newport Pagnell and its immediate vicinity.

Joseph Staines

The History of Newport Pagnell and its immediate vicinity.

Staines, Joseph
British Library, Historical Print Editions
British Library
1842
8°.
10360.ff.2.

The BiblioLife Network

This project was made possible in part by the BiblioLife Network (BLN), a project aimed at addressing some of the huge challenges facing book preservationists around the world. The BLN includes libraries, library networks, archives, subject matter experts, online communities and library service providers. We believe every book ever published should be available as a high-quality print reproduction; printed on- demand anywhere in the world. This insures the ongoing accessibility of the content and helps generate sustainable revenue for the libraries and organizations that work to preserve these important materials.

The following book is in the "public domain" and represents an authentic reproduction of the text as printed by the original publisher. While we have attempted to accurately maintain the integrity of the original work, there are sometimes problems with the original book or micro-film from which the books were digitized. This can result in minor errors in reproduction. Possible imperfections include missing and blurred pages, poor pictures, markings and other reproduction issues beyond our control. Because this work is culturally important, we have made it available as part of our commitment to protecting, preserving, and promoting the world's literature.

GUIDE TO FOLD-OUTS, MAPS and OVERSIZED IMAGES

In an online database, page images do not need to conform to the size restrictions found in a printed book. When converting these images back into a printed bound book, the page sizes are standardized in ways that maintain the detail of the original. For large images, such as fold-out maps, the original page image is split into two or more pages.

Guidelines used to determine the split of oversize pages:

• Some images are split vertically; large images require vertical and horizontal splits.
• For horizontal splits, the content is split left to right.
• For vertical splits, the content is split from top to bottom.
• For both vertical and horizontal splits, the image is processed from top left to bottom right.

HISTORY

OF

NEWPORT PAGNELL.

THE

HISTORY

OF

NEWPORT PAGNELL,

AND

ITS IMMEDIATE VICINITY.

BY JOSEPH STAINES.

Entered at Stationers' Hall.

NEWPORT PAGNELL:
PRINTED AND PUBLISHED BY C. TITE.
LONDON: HOULSTON AND STONEMAN, 65, PATERNOSTER ROW.
1842.

TO

WILLIAM TYRINGHAM PRAED, ESQUIRE,

MEMBER OF PARLIAMENT

FOR THE

BOROUGH OF SAINT IVES, CORNWALL,

AND

PRESIDENT OF THE NEWPORT PAGNELL BANK
FOR SAVINGS,

THESE MEMORIALS,

OF A TOWN ON WHICH HIS FAMILY HAVE FOR SEVERAL CENTURIES
CONFERRED MANY OBLIGATIONS, FROM THE REMOTE PERIOD
WHEN

HIS GENEROUS ANCESTOR LIBERALLY ADDED TO THE
ENDOWMENTS OF

THE PRIORY AT TICKFORD,

DOWN TO THE PRESENT TIME, ARE RESPECTFULLY

Dedicated,

BY HIS MOST OBLIGED

AND OBEDIENT SERVANT,

JOSEPH STAINES.

ADVERTISEMENT.

It was originally intended to insert at length, the authorities which have been consulted in the compilation of these pages; but, lest this should seem like a needless parade of research, that design was abandoned; and the Writer trusts that his readers will be content with the assurance, that he has been scrupulously exact in the collection and arrangement of the materials which have come within his reach.

The anxieties necessarily attending a publication of this kind, have been greatly relieved by the kindness shewn to the Writer during the progress of his work, and the assistance so generously afforded him by two or three of his friends, to whom he feels under special and peculiar obligation.

Those acquainted with the limited circulation of the history of a small town, will not be surprised that the work does not contain more pictorial illustration; it is however hoped, that the View of the Town from the Northampton Road, lithographed from an original painting, may meet with the approval of the Subscribers.

The Writer is fully aware that those who presume to appear before the public have no right to urge an indulgent consideration of their labours; but he craves permission to state, that in writing the History of Newport Pagnell, he has trodden an unbeaten path; and is fearful that many imperfections, will be found in his work.

This small volume has been compiled in those leisure hours only, which could be spared from the duties and engagements of a life devoted to the claims of business.

Savings' Bank,
  Newport Pagnell,
    30th November, 1842.

THE

HISTORY

OF

NEWPORT PAGNELL.

THE student of history has already learned to his cost, that the origin of our towns as well as that of our nation, is enveloped in darkness and obscurity; the stream of history has been so corrupted by the tributary streams of tradition, that to separate the truth from fable eludes the observation of the most untiring research. History is altogether silent as to the period when Britain first became inhabited: on a subject of such high antiquity she does not so much as "mumble her oracles;" it may be that the world was then young, and

"History, not wanted yet,
Lean'd on her elbow, watching Time, whose course,
Eventful, should supply her with a theme,"

B

Early
History.

Nor have we more certain information on the interesting subject of the origin and formation of our more ancient towns, for while erecting their mud-wall tenements it never entered the imagination of the most sanguine of our brave but unlettered ancestors, that the genius of England would one day give to their humble dwellings the lasting perpetuity of marble, and that in the ages to come the history of their earliest settlements would not only possess a value as interesting in itself, but doubly so as affording a running commentary on the history and characteristics of our country.

Ancient
Britons.

Prior to the Christian Era we know but little more, than that the tract of country in which the northern part of this county is situated, was populated by the Catieuchlani, a race of men whom the learned Camden supposes were descendants of the ancient Cassii, a term implying warlike valour; on which account it is probable that the Ancient Britons were called " the seed of Warriors."* The Catieuchlani being a powerful race, subjected to their power many of the Dobuni, who resided in the part now form-

---

* Cæsar speaks of the Ancient Britons as Barbarians; but the military discipline and war chariot noticed by him, shew that our Ancestors were not entirely uncivilized; and if Galgacus spoke in the manner described by Tacitus, that people could not be altogether rude whom such eloquence impressed.

ing the counties of Oxford and Gloucester; in their turn they were however expelled, by the arms of all-conquering Rome.

It was about half a century before the advent B. C. 55. of our Lord, when the Romans first invaded the Roman Invasion. shores of Britain. During their continuance here, they apportioned the kingdom into divisions, giving to this locality the name of *Cæsariensis Maxima*. BAXTER considers Lathbury* to have been the Lactodorum mentioned by Antoninus, and it is likely that Newport was included under the same name, as Roman coins have frequently been found in the Nursery Ground in Marsh End, as well as in the garden of Lathbury House; at all events there was a station here, and a road by the Kickles Farm, (where Roman antiquities have been frequently discovered,) which was probably continued through Hartwell to the neighbourhood of Northampton.

For some years after the departure of the A. D. 420. Romans we have to grope our way in the dark, and know but little of even the general condition of the country, but society must have made

---

* It has been suggested whether Bunstye, which is in the parish of Lathbury though beyond Gayhurst Wood, was not the place spoken of by Antoninus; that Bunstye was once a most important place, and gave its name to the Hundred no doubt can be entertained. In Domesday it is Benestou Hundred.

The Hep-
tarchy. advances; the machinery of government was improved, and the heptarchy, a seven-fold government, was constituted; this neighbourhood form-
ing a part of the Kingdom of Mercia, and so
continuing until the seven Crowns of England
centred on the head of Egbert, when that monarch swayed his sceptre over the length and
breadth of England.

A. D. 815,
Formation
of Towns
Centuries before this period towns had been
formed, thus affording to the populace "the
sweet security of streets." In selecting suitable
spots for their locality, proximity to water must
have frequently determined the choice; this advantage the site of our town afforded; its two
rivers, the Ouze and Lovatt, have been thus me-
morialised in ancient song.

> From Brackley breaking forth, through soils most
>   heavenly sweet,
> By Buckingham makes on and crosses Watling Street,
> She with her lesser Ouze* at Newport next doth twine,
> Which from proud Chiltern neare comes eas'ly ambling in.

The Saxons.
But whether Newport is of Roman or Saxon
origin, it is certain that not only at so early a
period as the union of the Heptarchy were the
foundations of our town laid, but the foundations of its commerce begun, for according to
an undisputed tradition, Egbert's grandson, the
great King Alfred, chartered four of the fairs.

* The Ouselle, sometimes called the Lovatt, or Willen river.

The earliest authentic record of Newport A.D. 1042. states, that our manor belonged to Ulf, a Thane of King Edward's, and that at the time of the survey it was held by William Fitz Ansculf. His father's name was Ansculf de Pinchengi or Pinkeney, who was the brother of Ghilo,* the ancestor of the baronial family of Pinkeney, of Weedon Pinkeney in Northamptonshire.

Doubts have been entertained whether Ans- Ansculf's culf was one of the Norman nobility. It has Origin. been supposed from the absence of his name both from the Domesday Lords and the roll of Battle Abbey, that he was a Saxon Noble ; and from his being named *Ans*culf, that he might have descended from Ulf, and through him acquired our manor†. It is curious that some hills on the banks of a lake near Newport

* He ranks as No. LII. in the Domesday Lords, and is there called Gilson.

† There is much yet unexplained mystery respecting this Saxon Noble. He is probably the same of whom Brooke Somerset Herald tells us, that on account of the difference likely to arise between his sons about the sharing of his Lands and Lordships after his death, he resolved to make them equal, and thereupon coming to York, with that horn wherewith he was used to drink, he filled it with wine, and kneeling devoutly before the Altar, drank the wine to God and St. Peter, prince of the Apostles, and by that ceremony enfeoffed the Church of York with all his lands and revenues. *Archæologia Vol. VI. Brown* 1782. *Mon. Rev.* 1784.

Ansculf.   in Shropshire (where this family had great possessions, and many of whose surrounding villages
bear the same name as ours) are called Ancs
Hills, and said to be so called from some Roman
Captain named Ancus that lay upon them, but
it seems much more probable that Ancus is a
corruption of Ansculf.*   This family is however
generally spoken of as being of Norman descent;
Mr. Hutton, the historian of Birmingham, a town
originally tributary to the same Lord as Newport,
says that Ansculf was one of William's Norman
followers, and Mr. Baker the well known historian of Northamptonshire, is of opinion that his
Norman origin will scarcely admit of a doubt. It
is probable that he was one of the Norman
Barons who were invited over to this country by
Edward the Confessor, and with his Son William
might possibly be in this kingdom to assist the
Norman Duke on his landing, while his brother
Ghilo it has been presumed came in with the
invading army.   The absence of his name
from the Domesday Lords, has been accounted
for upon the supposition of his decease prior to
its compilation, but upon careful examination it
will be found that his name does appear in
Domesday, as having by the command of King
William re-exchanged the moiety of Ellesborough
for Risborough ;† and as having disseized William

---

* Is our own " Ash Hill," a similar corruption ?

† In Elesberie hundred. Esenberge, [Ellesborough] Earl

de Celci of his lands at Bradwell.* Nor does the omission of his name in the roll of Battle Abbey, disprove his Norman birth, as the most eminent, indeed the father of Antiquaries considered the roll a doubtful, if not suspicious authority.

DUGDALE and the highest authorities agree in the statement that the Conqueror "bestowed upon William Fitz Ansculf, vast possessions of the disherited English," and it is the fact of these grants, that dispose us to the opinion of his Norman origin, for it was by the bestowal of our lands upon the favorites of his court, and the dependents on his fortune, (thus implanting his Norman Nobles on English soil,) that he hoped to maintain his title to the throne. The promise of these grants, roused in his cause the energies of his Nobles, and by their bestowal, he invigorated their drooping spirits and rewarded their fidelity. At the time of the survey Fitz Ansculf held eighty-six Lordships and Manors, and of all his

His supposed Norman birth.

Harold held this Manor and Ansculf de Pinchengi exchanged this Manor for half of Risenbergam, [Risborough] with (contr) Ralph Tailgebosch, by the command of King William. *Orig.* 148. *b.* 1.

* While Sheriff of this County, Ansculf disseized William de Celci of his lands at Bradwell, but, as was said by the men of Segelai Hundred, wrongfully and without the delivery of the King or of any other person. *Orig.* 149. *a.* 1.

Ansculf's
Castle.

possessions in this county* ours was the most valuable. The Castle of Dudley, one of the most ancient in the kingdom, having been erected about the year 700 by Dudo a Saxon, and so called from him, was Ansculf's principal seat, and was the head of his barony.

A. D. 1081.
Domesday
survey.

Newport, (it had not then its affix Pagnell,) at the time of the survey was entered as follows in the Domesday Book. *Nevport.* XIII. The land of the Earl of Moreton.† In Segelai Hundred.‡ In Caldecote, Alured holds of the Earl four hides§ and one virgate for one manor.

---

* His other possessions laid in Ellesborough, Haddenham, Ditton, Stoke, North Marston, Hoggeston, Soulbury, Hollington, Littlecot, Cheddington, Swanbourne, Marsh Gibbon, Woolstone, Bradwell, Linford, and Tyringham.

† Or Mortaigne. He was captured at the battle of Tenchebrai in 1106, he was confined in the Tower of London, and in the accounts of the Sheriffs of the City are the following entries :—In the livery of the Earl of Moreton £12. 12s. 6d. by tale, and for clothes for the sd. Earl 65s. by tale. *Pipe Roll* 31 *H.* 1. He ranks XIII in the Domesday Lords, next below the King, Bishops, and Abbots.

‡ Orig. 146. b. 2.

§ Hida and Caracuta, which frequently occur in Domesday, have hitherto been considered synonymous terms. Mr. Wyndham's conjecture respecting them, viz. " that the first was intended to signify the valuation of the Estate" and the latter " ye measurement of the Land," is founded on a nice attention to the subject before him, and is very clearly right. *Wyndham's Wiltshire* 1788. *Mon. Rev.* *June* 1790.

There is land to four ploughs. There is one Caldecote. and a half in the demesne,* and a half may yet be made. There are two vavasors† there, who pay thirty-two shillings and sixpence ; and one villane and five bordars‡ with two ploughs. There is one bondman,§ and one mill of five ores‖ and fourpence. Meadow for two ploughs.¶ Pannage for twenty-four hogs, and twenty-eight pence for custom; its whole value is, and always was four pounds. Four Thanes held this manor in King Edward's time, and might sell it and give it to whom they would. Caldecote continued. XVIII. Land of William son of Ansculf. In Segelai Hundred.** William holds three hides and one virgate in Caldecote. There is land to two ploughs. There is one in the demesne and another may be made. There is one villane and one mill of eight shillings, and a

---

* The Lord's chief manor place, in his own occupation. *Jacob*

† In dignity next a Baron. *Ibid.*

‡ Villane and Bordars appear to have been somewhat like our husbandmen or cottagers.

§ Bound to the person of the Lord. *Jacob.*

‖ This was Saxon money or coin, valued at sixteen pence, and sometimes, according to variation of the standard, at twenty-pence. It is a word which often occurs in Domesday, and the laws of King Canutus. A slave bought of the Abbots and Monks of Bath, his own liberty and that of his children for five *Orcs*, (about four shillings and eightpence halfpenny,) and twelve sheep. *Mon. Rev. July* 1786.

¶ A term of measurement. ** Orig. 148, 149. b. 1.

Caldecote concluded. certain Knight has there half a hide with half a plough. Meadow for one plough. Pannage for one hundred hogs. It is and was always worth forty shillings. Two vassals of Vlfs held this manor and might sell it. Caldecote concluded. LVIII. Land of Lewin de Neweham. Suarting holds two hides and half in Caldecote. There is land to one plough. There is one there and another may be made. One hide and a half are in the demense. There are two bordars, and meadow for one plough. It is and was always worth twenty shillings. Gonni, a vassal of Alurics, the son of Goding, held this land and

Newport Manor

might sell it. XVIII. Land of William son of Ansculf. In Segelai Hundred.* Manor. William himself holds *Nevport*. It answered for five hides. There is land to nine ploughs. There are four carucates of land in the demesne and there are four ploughs there; and five Villanes have five ploughs. The Burgesses‡ have six ploughs and a half, and of other vassals not working upon the five hides. [aliorumque ho-

---

* Orig. 149. a. 1.

‡ Men of trade, inhabitants of a Borough or walled Town. That the term was not exclusively used to distinguish the inhabitants of a town returning Members to Parliament, no greater proof can be produced than the fact that at this time Parliament was not in existence, nor at any subsequent period does Newport appear in the ancient Summonses to Parliament.

minum Ext. v. hid. laborantes.] There are nine bondmen and two mills of forty shillings. Meadow for all the ploughs and ten shillings. Pannage for three hundred hogs, and two shillings, and moreover four shillings from the Vassals who dwell in the wood, and for all other rents it pays yearly, one hundred shillings, and sixteen shillings, and four-pence. Its whole value is twenty pounds, and it was worth in King Edward's time twenty-four pounds, Vlf a Thane of King Edward's held this manor. XVIII. Land of William son of Ansculf. In Mosleie Hundred. Manor. William himself holds Ticheforde. It answered for five hides. There is land to eight ploughs. Besides these five hides, there are in the demesne two carucates of land, and two ploughs therein. Six villanes with four Bondmen, have there six ploughs. Meadow for five ploughs. Pannage for fifty hogs. Five Sokemen* there, pay twenty seven shillings. It is worth one hundred shillings;† when received six pounds, and the same in King Edward's time. Vlf, a Thane of King Edward's, held this manor, and there were five Thanes who held three virgates and a half of

---

* Tenants who held their lands, to plough the land of their Lords with their own ploughs. *Jacob.*

† A shilling was equal in weight of silver to nearly three times the same amount in modern money, and in efficiency to a much greater sum.

this land, and they might sell to whom they would.

The survey for the compilation of Domesday, which occupied five years, was concluded in 1086, since which time the parish of Newport has undergone so many changes, that we cannot trace all the property as therein described.   Little Linford Wood, may be at least some remains of the wood in which the Vassals resided, as at that time Little Linford, though now a separate parish, was a Chapelry to Newport.   It is probable that the land occupied by the Burgesses, (which appears to have been considerable,) was as the name would seem to imply Port Field, whether Bury Field was included cannot be ascertained; but if, as the learned Camden states, bury is a corruption of burgh, we are lead to the impression that such was the case.   Terms however are of various application, for the term port does not invariably mean a sea coast town, its Saxon signification is a town or city, and thus those lands occupied by the Burgesses, might have obtained the distinction of the port, that is, the *town* field; nor is it altogether unworthy of consideration, whether this town itself did not acquire the name of the New *Port*, [Town,] while the ancient town of Bonstye, was gradually sinking into decay and ruin.

But to return to the course of our history, William Ansculf had according to Edmonson no

Margin notes:
Little Linford Wood.

Port Field.

male issue to survive him, leaving an only daugh- Paganell's
ter Beatrix, who married Sir Fulk Paganell, noble descent.
the possessions therefore which she acquired
through her father (and as we have already stated
they were considerable) passed into the Knight's
hands.   The Knight was of honourable and
noble descent, his father was one of those Norman
Barons on whom the Conquorer had bestowed
the most princely grants, for at the time of the
survey he held ten lordships in Devonshire, five
in Somerset, fifteen in Lincoln, and fifteen in
Yorkshire ; and in the second of William Rufus, A. D. 1089.
he founded and endowed the Priory of the Holy
Trinity, in the city of York.   His son the Knight,
emulous of following his father's good and pious
example, laid on the altar of the Church, his
thank-offering for benefits received. In the same,*
or according to others, the following reign, he
founded the Priory at Tickford in this parish, Tickford
and gave thereto the Church of Newport with Priory founded.
its appurtenances, and with a munificence which
eclipses the liberality of the present day, added
to the endowment, the Churches and Lordships
of Bradwell, Willien, and Chicheley, the mill at
Caldecote, and half a yard of land, with the
meadow which belongs to the mill,† and some
property in Northamptonshire.‡   The Priory

* Dug. Mon.   † Ibid, Vol. II. 910.
‡ It has been stated, that the Chapel of Linford Parva
was also given to the Priory ; but Great Linford, and Little

was of the order of Saint Bennett, or as it was afterwards called Cluniack Monks, the richest in Europe, and the number of whose houses in England was twenty seven.* These Monks were called Black Monks, as when abroad they wore over their other garments a black hood and cloak; they were of the order of preaching Friars, the conversion of hereticks being their peculiar province. And here, to prevent confusion, it may be proper to state, that throughout our history the terms Abbey, Priory, Convent, and Monastery, will be used indiscriminately, for though there were shades of difference, they are not easily to be distinguished.

There are however, two distinctive terms which must be clearly understood as we pass on in our history. This Priory in common with many others, was under the controul of a house of greater eminence, and therefore called a " Cell," and as this superior house (to use the phraseology of the day) was "a house beyond the seas;"

Linford, with Carfax Church, Oxford, were given by Canute in 1032, to the Benedictines of St. Mary at Abingdon, as appears in the Charter of Confirmation, which is still preserved.

* The Cluniacks were a reform of St. Bennett's order, the first institutor of which, was Abbot Berno; to whom William, then Duke of Aquitain, gave the place called "Clugny" in Burgundy, for their first habitation. Anno. 890. *Grey's Eccle. Law*, p. 441.

our Abbey had yet one other distinction it was an "Alien" Priory. The superior house was the Monastery of Saint Martin, (Marmoustier) at Tours in Normandy, many of whose Monks came to reside in this country, and were domiciled by William in the Abbey erected in celebration of the victory won at Hastings, whose high altar was on the spot where Harold had planted his standard and hence called Battle Abbey. *Battle Abbey.*

Ralph Paganell, to whom Newport had now descended, was one of the powerful faction of Barons, who in their adherence to the Empress Maud, went so far as openly to renounce their allegiance to their Sovereign. He held amongst others the castle at Ludlow, and Stephen having subdued many of his opponents at length sat down before this castle, but the garrison made so vigorous a defence as to compel the king to convert the siege into a blockade. Prince Henry of Scotland, who was with Stephen, having ventured too near the enemy's works, was dragged from his horse by a grappling-hook, and was rescued from his perilous situation by Stephen, in a manner which afforded a signal instance of the King's courage and humanity. In the mean time Gervase, Ralph's son, was holding his father's castle at Dudley on behalf of the same cause. *A.D. 1133.* *Ludlow Castle.*

On the death of Ralph, Gervase confirmed the grants of his father and grandfather to Tickford Priory, adding thereunto the church of Aston juxta Birmingham, and founded and endowed a Priory at Dudley.

Dudley Castle.

A daughter of Henry II., in the twelfth year of her father's reign, was married to a foreigner, and as she had resided at Dudley, might possibly be married at the castle. Gervase's assessment of aid,* common in those days on the marriage of a king's daughter, was proportionate to his wealth and establishment. It might be that a grateful recollection of his hospitality on this interesting occasion, as well as a memorial of the important services rendered to the Empress Maud his mother, induced the king to confer, as he did, on the Priory of Tickford the power of punishing criminals.

A.D. 1187. Geoffry Tyringham

In the 33rd of this reign Geoffry Tyringham bestowed a substantial testimony of his regard to Tickford Abbey, by adding to its endowments the church at Tyringham ;† seventeen years before which, the manor of Tyringham had become the property of the family bearing that name.

In the first of Richard I.,‡ Gervase Paganell was one of the Barons attending the first solemn coronation of Richard, that monarch having been

---

* He certified his Knight's fees to be fifty de veteri feoffamento, and these de novo, six and a third part.

† Tyringham appears to have been called " Tedlingham" at the time of the survey.

‡ Paynell or Pagnell, William, } are included in the list
————————————Thomas, } of such of the English Nobility and Gentry as went on the Crusades in this reign.

crowned three times. He married Isabel, daugh- Gervase Paganell.
ter of Robert Earl of Leicester, and widow of
Simon Saint Liz, Earl of Northampton, and of
Huntingdon, by whom Paganell had issue two
sons, Robert and Gervase, who probably died
young, as Hawyse his daughter became his sole
heiress, and married first, John de Somerie or
Sumerie, and afterwards Roger de Berkeley, of
Berkeley in the county of Gloucester; Leicester was deputed by the Barons assembled at
Northampton in 1164 to read the sentence of
imprisonment to Thomas á Beckett, and a descendant of the Berkeleys lately resided in this
neighbourhood.

The family of Paganell having now merged The affix Pagnell
in that of Somerie, it is natural to suppose that
Pagnell, however derived, became an affix to
Newport through its connection with that family;
and there being another Newport it would seem
desirable to distinguish by some term this town
from the Newport in Shropshire, in both of
which towns it will be remembered this family
had great possessions. Two reasons have been
assigned why Pagnell was affixed to Newport.
There is a popular tradition that the affix is derived
from two daughters of Paganell, Margaret and
Eleanor, who were joined together at their birth;
and it is said that Pag Nell is a corruption of
Peg, and Nell, the common abbreviation of

Tradition. Margaret and Eleanor; it is further said that these ladies were considerable benefactresses to the town, Buryfield being amongst the number of their gifts; and that the two brass effigies which were on the floor of the nave of the parish church, were sacred to their memory. The other reason is that assigned by Camden, that Newport *Paynel* is so called from the Lord of the Manor, Fulk Paganell.

Which of these is the correct opinion, may seem, as indeed it is, of but trifling importance; but in a professed History of the Town, it may not be improper to glance at the evidence adduced in support of each opinion. The main question From whom did these ladies descend? can never now be answered. The family pedigree preserved by Dugdale, and one prepared by consulting the highest antiquarian authorities, does not bear the name of either Margaret or Eleanor; and even if their names had appeared, that alone would not have been satisfactory; nor is the evidence afforded by the brass effigies more conclusive.

Upon an inspection of the remaining brass,* (the

---

* It is probable that these effigies are those spoken of by Cole, as belonging to one of the family of St. Leger, who was buried in the church in 1447. A correspondent (Lathburiensis) in the Gentleman's Magazine, suggests that the effigies were those of Sir George St. Leger, who died about 1547, and that the date 1447 is an error of Cole's transcriber.

other was stolen by the old sexton, for which Brass offence he was flogged round the town) it does not effigy. appear to belong to the age of Anglo Norman ladies; the dress not corresponding with the costume of that period. But it is hardly within the range of possibility that these brasses should belong to any of the Paganells who were connected with this town; as effigies of this kind, are in no case of higher antiquity than that of the reign of Henry II.; and the Lysons's state that the most ancient authenticated brass effigy in this county is of the year 1373, the close of the reign of Henry III., a century after the Manor of Newport had passed from the Paganells.

There is a Court in Silver-street called the The Paggs Paggs, but the tradition respecting it that these Court ladies resided there, is of that equally vague character with other portions of the tradition, for the family though they might occasionally reside, do not appear to have been regularly seated here, but at Boothby Pagnell, in Lincolnshire. Whether Bury Field was the gift of any of this family, either male or female, is a matter not likely now to be brought to light, even though the Archives of Rome were searched, where it is said the original deeds were deposited. It cannot but be admitted, that there are many objections to the idea of this property having been derived from any female descendant of the Paganells; and upon the whole, it would appear that Bury Field

was a portion of the land occupied by the burgesses alluded to in Domesday Book.   With
these difficulties then meeting us at every turn,
we have no choice but to discard the long told
tradition, cherished as it may have been, and
come to the more rational conclusion assigned
by Camden, that Newport Pagnell is so called
from the Lord of it, Fulk Paganell.   And in
corroboration of this opinion, let us call to
mind Fulk Paganell's princely munificence in
founding and endowing our Priory ; an act which
would secure to him the gratitude and respect of
the neighbourhood ; and out of compliment to
him, and to connect his name with that land
which he had so nobly devoted to the service of
the Church, his dependents might perchance
add Pagnell to the name of Newport, an honourable and legitimate tribute to the benevolence and
piety of a man so well deserving this lasting
memorial.   The addition of a name through
its Lord, is one of not unfrequent occurence :
in illustration of which, we may instance the
neighbouring village of Milton, which, as is
well authenticated derives its additional name
Keynes, from the ancient family of Keynes, who
possessed the Manor, one of whom, William de
Keynes, was the Knight* who took King Stephen

marginal notes:
Affix de-
rived from
its Lord.

Milton
Keynes.

* Our modern histories state this fact somewhat differently.   The old chroniclers say Keynes took the King
prisoner, but that Stephen refused to make a *formal* sur-

prisoner at the battle of Lincoln. There are A.D. 1141.
besides Newport, three other towns bearing the Hootone Pagnell.
affix Pagnell. Hootone *Pagnell* in Yorkshire, of
which Manor Paganell was the Lord, and which
with the Church and all other things thereunto
appertaining, he had given to the house of the
Holy Trinity at York; Boothby Pagnell in Lincolnshire, and Littleton Painell in Wiltshire:
respecting the former, there is no such absurd
tradition accounting for the additional name as
we have, the general opinion being, that it is derived from its connection with the Paganells.

While this country was governed by the Princes Newport Castle.
of the Norman line, it was generally in a most
unsettled state, and order could only be maintained by the military retainers of the Barons
who resided in their castles. According to the
custom of the age, Newport was fortified by a
castle; and, as similar erections existed at Laven-
don, Wolverton, and that part of Hanslope now
called " Castle" Thorpe, this neighbourhood
must have been one of the most formidable posi-
tions in the kingdom; nor does it appear to
have been disturbed by insurrections.

It is likely that the castle was erected soon
after the Conquest; for William found the fortresses which had been erected by the Romans

render to a Knight, whereupon the Earl of Gloucester, who
was in the field, was summoned, and to him the King resigned his sword.

and Saxons so few in number, and those in so
decayed a state, that but little more than their
ruins remained; and to guard against invasion
from enemies without, and tumult from foes within,
he at once began to erect castles all over the
kingdom. The turbulent state of the country
afterwards, occasioned a rapid increase; for in
the reign of Stephen they amounted to the number of 1115, averaging twenty-seven for each
county. The site of the Castle is still distinctly
visible at the point where the two rivers meet.*
The Lovatt is said to have formed a moat to that
part which faced the meadow, called even in the

---

* The favourite situation of Castles was, for the sake of
security, an eminence on the bank of a river. Dungeon
Lane is said to have been a private road by which prisoners
of war were conducted to the *donjon* of the Castle, without
passing through the principal street; and it is remarkable,
that at Odell in Bedfordshire, there is a Lane similarly situated, bearing the same name, which was also a private road
leading to that Castle. Sir Walter Scott in his notes to
Marmion, states that the *donjon*, in its proper signification,
means the strongest part of a feudal castle; a high square
tower, with walls of tremendous thickness, situated in the
centre of the other buildings, from which, however, it was
usually detached. Here, in case of the outward defences
being gained, the garrison retreated to make their last stand.
The donjon contained the great hall, and principal rooms of
state for solemn occasions, and also the prison of the fortress;
from which last circumstance we derive the modern and re-
stricted use of the word *dungeon*.

time of Edward II., Castle meadow.† The pre- Newport
Castle.
sent state of the ground, probably much altered
during the civil wars, renders it impossible to
decide whether it was a Castle for residence as
well as defence; could we but arrive at this
fact, we should at once have some clue to the
time of its erection. Castles of residence, being
according to Boswell, in no case of higher antiquity than the reign of William I.

In process of time, Castles became of little use
as fortresses; the more settled state of the country, the abolition of the feudal system, and more
particularly the discovery of gunpowder, having
occasioned a total change in the art of war, rendered these places of strength of much less importance. These circumstances (together with
the fact of Roger de Somerie building a Castle
at Bordesley, which afterwards became his principal seat) led to the neglect of the Castle at
Newport; and though it ultimately became a
prey to the unsparing ravages of time, we do
not know upon what authority it has been
stated, that there were no ruins of it in existence in Camden's time. Camden in his Camden.
Magna Britannica, (to collect materials for which
that celebrated man travelled through the kingdom, publishing the result of his labours in the
reign of Elizabeth) speaking of Newport *Paynel*,
simply states that " John de Somerie had his

† Charter of Confirmation, 5th Edward II.

Castle here;" and from this expression, it would appear that topographers, following each others steps, have at once concluded that not even its ruins were then in existence: they seemed to have overlooked a remark which the father of antiquaries has made in the body of his work, that his design did not permit of his adverting to every Castle which had come under his notice.

Leland also refers to the Castle in his manuscript collection, preserved in the Bodleian Library.

There can be little doubt but that the Castle *John de Somerie.* was the residence of John de Somerie, who married the last Paganell; the Baron did not live long to enjoy his newly acquired possession, which descended to his son Ralph, of whom it is said that he "had seizin of the Barony of Gervase *A.D. 1210.* Paganell."* Ralph died in the 11th of the reign of John, when his son William became the Lord of the Manor of Newport, about which period the Castle of Hanslope was destroyed.

A.D. 1215. *Magna Charta.* William's youth, when the tomb closed over his father, renders it unlikely that he should have joined the Barons in their memorable and effective struggle for Magna Charta; but as we do not know his age when he died, he might have been amongst their number; but few of their names have been handed down; for it is useless, said the old chroniclers, to enumerate the Barons who composed the army of God, and of holy Church,

* Banks.

they were the whole nobility of England. William dying in 1222, and his only son Nicholas surviving his father but seven years, this Manor and the Barony of Dudley passed to Roger de Somerie, a younger brother of William.

Previous to the year 1240, an Hospital dedicated to Saint Margaret had been founded here, and it was during this year, it is said, that a second Hospital was erected. St. Margaret's hospital.

In the contentions between Henry III. and some of his Barons, Roger de Somerie stoutly adhered to the King, and was with him taken prisoner on the 14th of May at the battle of Lewes; a circumstance which might induce the King to grant a Market to the town, and a Fair of eight days, commencing on the festival of Saint Luke, being the 18th of October; though by some it is said that the grant of the Market was only confirmed by the King. Roger de Somerie. A. D. 1264.

It has been asserted that Roger de Somerie having neglected to obey a summons to receive the order of Knighthood, was dispossessed of his lands by Henry, and that they were granted to Walter de Kirkham for his life; this statement however wants confirmation; it is true that the character of Henry, with the trying situation in which he was placed, together with his known treatment of others who like this Baron were his personal friends, does not render such arbitrary proceedings at all improbable, yet on the

E

Roger de Somerie.

other hand, Dugdale and Banks are silent upon the subject; if Roger de Somerie was dispossessed, his lands must have been soon restored, as all authorities agree that shortly afterwards they were in the possession of his family.*

St. John's Hospital. A. D. 1287.

We find upon the authority of Browne Willis, that seven years after the decease of Roger de Somerie, who died in 1280, John de Somerie, a brother of Roger, the then Lord, instituted an hospital dedicated to Saint John the Baptist, and Saint John the Evangelist; Speed however, describes St. John's hospital as founded by John de Peynton of this place, but it is probable it was jointly endowed by him and Roger de Somerie; Speed also asserts that it was dedicated to Saint Leonard, but it may be presumed from the fact of the date of its foundation and its value at the dissolution being the same, that it was but one house.

This hospital designed for "*leprose*" or sick persons, was erected on the site occupied by the present hospital, for houses of this kind were generally built on the road-side, being also intended for the relief of travellers. The patients had generally with them two or three "*religious*" (a term used in designating the inmates of a religious house) a Chaplain and a Master or Prior,

* "The bondmen of our beloved and faithful John de Somerie, *now* Lord of Newport. *The Charter of Confirmation.*

who were empowered by Letters Patent, to receive gifts and grants.

In the reign of Edward I., an Inquisition Inquisition
was taken on the oath of seventeen men before
the King's Escheator, which sets out a full extent
of the Manor of Newport, and contains very
minutely and distinctly, every description of possession connected therewith; it gives the quantity, quality, and price of the land, meadows,
pasture, underwood, and mills, with the rent of
the Burgesses, and the tolls of the market. It
was during this reign Sir Roger Tyringham at- Sir Roger
tended the King on his mission to Scotland, when Tyringham
A. D. 1291.
he decided the controversy between the rival
claimants to the throne of that kingdom.

The rolls of Parliament of the thirtieth of
Edward I., record the following curious fact re- A. D. 1302.
specting Sir William *Pannel*, which reflects but Sir William
little credit on the parties concerned. Sir William Pannel.
purchased, strange as it may seem, the wife of
John de Camois, the son of Ralph, Lord Camois,
who in the words of the deed of conveyance which
he sealed before many witnesses, " out of his own
free will, gave and demised his own wife Margaret, (daughter and heir of John de Gadsden) to
Sir William Pannel, Knight; and to the same
William voluntarily, gave, granted, released, and
quit claimed, all the goods and chattels which
she hath, or otherwise hereafter might have, and
also whatsoever was in his hands of the aforesaid

Sir William Pannel. Margaret's goods and chattels, with their appurtenances, so that neither he himself nor any man
else in his name, might claim or challenge any
interest, nor ought for ever, in the aforesaid
Margaret, or in the goods and chattels of the
said Margaret."

On the death of Camois, Margaret was married
to Sir William Pannel, and by petition in Parliament, laid claim to the third part of her former
husband's estate as her dower; this claim being
resisted, a long suit was the result, of which both
Camden and Dugdale speak as being very famous
in its time. But a woman who could forget the
vows which were upon her, and should be a con-
senting party to her transfer to another, could
surely have no claim upon the estates of her former
husband for her dower; and such was the solemn
decision of Parliament, for we find that judgment
was very properly given against her.*

* The circumstances narrated in the text, are of a nature
so extraordinary, that the following additional facts may not
prove uninteresting to some of our readers. In reply to
the Claimant's petition, the Defendant pleaded an elopement, and that she had lived as an adultress with the
Demandant; he replied that her husband granted her to
him in his lifetime, virtute cujus non vixit ut Adultera,
with the Demandant, Sir William, but as his wife; and upon
demurrer to this replication, judgment was given against
him under the statute of William II.; it being determined,
1. That it was a void grant. 2. That it did not amount to
a license. 3. That after elopement there should not be any

We meet only in two or three other instances The Paga-
with the name of *Paynell* or *Painell*. Two nells.
Knights, William and Fulk, who about the year
1230, proposed the invasion of Normandy; a John,
Lord Painell, held property in Wiltshire, at Littleton Painell, so called from him; and at a much
later period, a Thomas Paynell, or Paganell, was
Canon regular, and afterwards Prior of Merton
Priory. He appears to have been a very pious
and learned man, and being ejected by Henry
VIII., he retired with a pension, passing his time
contentedly between London and Oxford, em-
ploying himself in writing or translating several
useful books.* There can be little doubt, that
each of these persons was a descendant of the
younger branches of the family of Gervase Paganell.

averment quod non fuit adulterium, though she married the
adulterer after her first husband's death. A sentence of
purgation of adultery in the Ecclesiastical Court was produced, but it was not allowed to have any effect.

This is the first judgment given on the statute, and is the
first and only instance of a wife being granted by deed.
The case was decided in the Parliament which assembled at
Lincoln the 29th Edward I., and closed their session at
Westminster the year following. *See.* 2—*Inst.*

* The Pandects of the Evangelical Law. 1553. Lond.
The Pithy and most notable Sayings of all the Scripture,
1560. Lond. Of the Contempt of the World, written by
Erasmus, 1533. Lond. A Sermon on the Lord's Prayer,
written by St. Cyprian, 1539. Salernus's Regimen of
Health, 1554. Lond., and some others.

Destruction   At the close of the 13th, or about the com-
of Tickford   mencement of the 14th century, the Priory was
Priory.
consumed by fire ; and together with its deeds
and charters totally destroyed. In consequence of
this, Edward II., in the 5th year of his reign, as the
Charter of   instrument sets forth, " by the influence of God,
Confirma-   favourably regarding the entreaties of the Prior,
tion.
and willing to do more ample grace to his well-
beloved brother in Christ, William de la Menerere,"
under the Great Seal witnessed at Northampton,
A. D. 1312.   on the 11th day of August, granted a Charter
of Confirmation, and it is from this document we
can alone ascertain what were the original possessions of the Abbey. The Charter after a recital of the loss which the Abbey had sustained,
informs us that " it was found by Inquisition
taken by the King's command, and returned into
his Chancery, that the founder of the Priory,
Fulk Paganell, gave to the Monks there, amongst
other possessions, the site of the same house ;
The Abbey   and all the land on both sides of the Monechus*
possessions   Street, extending from the gate of the same house,
to the cross next the highway leading towards
London ; and all the lands and tenements in the
street called Hawe† street, to the bridge of Tykeford ; and also a certain meadow called the Castle

---

* In ancient documents this street is called " Monk-
house-street," an evident corruption from Monechus-street.
It is now called Abbey End.

          † Now called Tickford End.

Mead; and a free and several fishery in the river Ouse, under the close of the same house from the corner of their Court upon the river called Le Ilvele, unto the ditch called Larke* brooke, towards the east; and the mill of Caldecote, and the pond of the same mill, with twenty-four and a half acres of land, and three acres of meadow, with the appurtenances in Tykeford, &c.; the tythe of Eels, and of the mill of Newport; pasture for twelve cows and one bull, in all his feedings and pastures in Newport, in the same places in which his oxen are depastured; the tythe of venison in his park at Tykeford, and also the meadow called the Hog Mead next their garden, and the mill-pond on the north side of Newport. And that the same Prior receive every year two marks in the name of a pension from the church of Bernak, by the hands of the Abbot of Peters-burgh [Peterborough] together with the ex-penses of every messenger seeking the two marks, as long as the said messenger shall make stay there expecting the pension; together with a Court Leete and Court Baron in Newport, Tyke-ford, Marsh,† Caldecote, Chichely, Thykethorn, and Hardmead;—and for amending the state of his Priory, we have granted to the Prior for us and our heirs, that he and his successors, Priors

* About midway between the Abbey and the Bridge at Sherington, there is still a ditch bearing that name.

† Marsh End.

of the same place, for ever may have in the
town of Tykeford, in his soil there, a Pillory
and a Tumberell, to punish and chastise trans-
gressors there, as shall be just."

Four years after the Charter of confirmation,
Writ and
Inquisition
9 Edw. II. we find a Writ and Inquisition (ad quod damnum)
taken before the King's Escheator,* giving the
King's permission to his beloved and faithful
Roger le Brabanzon, Henry Spigurnell, John de
Somerie, William and Robert de Wenrich, and
Martin le Engleys, to give and assign divers property to his beloved in Christ, the Prior and
Convent of Tickford, next Newport Pannel.
Somerie's gift was a right of certain fisheries " in
the water of Lovente, from the bridge of Tickford
to the fisheries of Mulsho and Willies," to be
held by the Priors and their successors in pure
and perpetual alms for ever; at the dissolution,
this right passed into other hands, and out of it
arose the celebrated law trial at Buckingham,
about the commencement of this present century.

We turn once more to the family of the Some-
A.D. 1323. ries : and we find that John, the fifth in descent,
died without issue, and that his estates were
divided between his two sisters; Dudley Castle
being apportioned to Margaret, the wife of John
de Sutton, and Newport Pagnell to Joan, the

---

* The Writ annexed to the Inquisition, is directed to
" His beloved clerk, Master John Walewayn, his Escheator
on this side Trent."

wife of Thomas de Botetourt, to whose descendant John, Edward III. confirmed the market.

On the death of these two ladies, the name of the Someries became extinct; for families however great and noble, pass into that oblivion to which the changes and chances of time are constantly and irretrievably consigning them; and now Newport *Pagnell* has only its affix and its Hospital, to tell of the Ansculfs, Paganells, and Someries of bye-gone days. Somerie's Castle does not exist even as a ruin, every vestige has been engulphed in the eddies of time; nor has a much better fate attended the Castle at Dudley Dudley,* some idea of whose original extent and Castle. magnificence can be conceived from the fact, that its dining table was one entire slab of oak, one yard wide, and five and twenty yards long; but the guests, who feasted so gaily around it, have risen, and departed never to return, for

> " The Knights are dust,
> Their swords are rust,
> And their good souls in paradise we trust."

The only memorial of any of these families

* The Castle stood on seven acres of ground; and from a report made to the Star Chamber in Charles I., we learn that it was in a perfect state of repair, fit to receive his Majesty, the Queen, and Prince at one time; the value of the woods amounted to £20,000., and the circuit of the Castle, Manors, Parks and Chase lying round it together, contained nineteen or twenty miles. *Tour through part of England. Mon. Rev. Mar.* 1778.

having been buried here, for Parish Registers are of a later date, that of Newport being commenced in 1548, is that of Browne Willis, who states that there are in the Church said to be brought from Tickford, the grave-stones robbed of their brasses of the Paganells of *Caphold.* "In the Priory Chapel at Dudley, there were several very remarkable monuments to the memory of the Someries who lay there; there was one especially, being cross-legged (the symbol of a Knight Templar) and a very old one, which, as it was a very goodly one for the workmanship, so it was much more strange for the stature of the person who was therein buried. I measured the picture which laid over him, says Erdeswicke,* and found it full eight feet long, neither was the person of lesser stature, for the coffin wherein the charnel was laid, being of free-stone, and hewed hollow, answerable to the proportions of a man, the hollow was also of eight feet, so that the body could be no less, for if it had, it could not with convenience have been laid in it." It is much to be regretted that there was no inscription, but the remains of a figure of a blue Lion prove at once that it must belong to one of the Someries. The sanctity and piety of one of the Roger de Someries, (perchance the gigantic Knight Templar) secured a signal honor being paid to his ashes; for the Bishop of

Dudley Priory.

* History of Staffordshire.

Coventry, the Diocesan of Dudley, granted forty day's indulgence to such as having confessed and communicated, should say one Ave in the Conventual Church of Dudley for the soul of Roger de Somerie, including the souls of all the faithful departed.

Edward III. who had so far benefited this town as to confirm its market, now laid his hands on the revenues of the Priory at Tickford. Edward's war with France (in which his son, the Black Prince, made himself illustrious, and the brave Sir Thomas D'Agworth, Lord of the Manor of Great Linford, perished by the sword) having drained his coffers, and the Parliament being unwilling to vote the necessary supplies, he was driven to other measures; and the Alien Priories of which there were an hundred and ten, having long excited the jealousy of the nation, the King availed himself of the opportunity of causing their suppression, and devoting their revenues to the service of the state. *Dissolution of Tickford Priory.*

The entire extinction of the religious houses, was a subject which was agitated in the reign of Henry IV., and the king was only prevented from adopting the proposed measure, by the remonstrance of the Clergy, through their organ the Archbishop Arundel. This distinguished Prelate, so acted upon the King's fears of violating his coronation oath,* as not only to *The General Dissolution proposed. A.D. 1422.*

* Such was the reason assigned by the King's friends;

deter Henry from taking this step, but was so far successful, as to prevail upon the King to surrender the revenues of the Alien Priories, which for some time past had been in the hands of the crown.

Restoration of Tickford Priory.

On its restoration, Tickford Abbey was made subservient, as it was fitting it should be, to the Priory of the Holy Trinity at York, which had been founded by the elder Paganell, so that though it continued to be a " *Cell,*" it was no longer an " *Alien*" Priory, Alien Priories having been entirely abolished.

Assizes held at Newport.

It was during the reign of Henry VI., that the assizes for the county, after having been occasionally held at Newport during the two preceding centuries, were altogether removed. In 1240-41, and again in 1249, it is supposed they were presided over by Galfridus de Gibbewin, who was Rector of Great Linford, and an Itinerant Justice; and his time being much occupied in his Itinerant Court and duties, might lead him by the Bishop's

but if his conscience was so tender on the subject of the violation of his oath, how is it that these scruples did not altogether deter him from taking that oath; the truth appears to be, that Henry was deeply sensible that he had no right to the throne, and he might hope that this surrender would make him popular, and so establish his usurped possession; and probably this concession was one of the causes which enabled the house of Lancaster to hold as " Kings de facto" the crown for half a century.

permission, to appoint in **1220**, a stipendary Vicar at Great Linford.*

In the meantime, Newport Manor passed from Botetourts. John de Botetourt, to his grand-daughter (in right of her father and brother) the lady of Sir Hugh Burnell. It is a disputed point whether this lady died without issue; at her death the Manor passed to the Berminghams it is said by marriage, but after long research, we have not been able to find the record of any such marriage.

The Berminghams were descendants of Peter Berming- de Bermingham, on whom Ralph Paganell be- hams. stowed the lordship of the now important town of Birmingham, as a reward for his faithful services as "Sewer to the said Gervase Paganell."†

From the Berminghams, the Manor passed by purchase to the Botelors, and towards the close Earl of Or- of the reign of Henry VI., it was in the possession mond. of James Botelor, Earl of Ormond, a prominent character in the wars of the rival Roses, when the gentle hills of England, glistened with hostile lances and hostile bands. The Earl was at the battle of St. Albans, where the Yorkists prevail- Wars of the ing, he fled, and escaped by casting his armour into Roses. a ditch. He survived the fate of many of the great and the noble at the " bloody fray at Wakefield,"

* Register at Lincoln.

† The Berminghams, Burnells, and Botetourts, as Barons of England, were summoned to Parliament.

but it was only to suffer, after the battle at Mortimer's Cross, an ignominious death by the hands of the public executioner, for he was taken prisoner at Touton, and suffered on the first of May at Newcastle. In the Parliament which met on the 4th of November, he was attainted, though dead when the manor of Newport reverted to the crown. Amongst the victims of Queen Margaret's relentless vengeance was Sir John Tyringham, who having fallen into her hands shared the fate of some of his companions in arms.

A.D. 1461.

Sir John Tyringham

In the following year, the manor became the property of that "thunder clap of war," Richard Neville Earl of Warwick, of whom it was said that he was the proud setter up and putter down of Kings, he retained the property until his death on the battle field at Barnet.*

Earl of Warwick.

A.D. 1472.

The manor of Newport once more changed hands, (earthly possessions at all times uncertain, were now more so through the violence of the times,) and became the property of George Duke of Clarence, (through his marriage with Warwick's daughter Isabel,) who by some Historians is said to have died in the tower; the more popular belief however being that his brothers, (Edward IV., and Richard III.) secretly

Duke of Clarence.

* The reader of Shakespeare (and who is not?) can hardly fail to be reminded of the affecting description of his death in the third part of Henry VI.

caused him to be drowned in a butt of Malmsey A.D.1479. wine.

Once more the manor reverted to the Crown, but was subsequently restored to the Saint Leg- St. Legers. ers, as being the representatives of the Botelers in the female line.

Before we proceed to detail the circumstances which led to the destruction of the Abbey at Tickford, we will give as complete a list of the Priors of Priors as can now be obtained. Tickford.

1187. Tobat de Bohun.
1210. Bernard.
1219. Hugh   resigned the next year to
1220. William, a Monk elected; at his resignation, John de Holna, a Monk of Spalding. was ad-mitted by the Bishop of Lincoln.
1259. Olliver presided.
1266. Gilbert, who resigned in
1267, and Bartholomew became Prior, at whose death in
1271. Reginald de Cossam was elected.
1275. Simon occurs as Prior.
1293. Gonfinders, who resigned in
1302. and William de Menevere was admitted none Julii resigned, 18 Cal Julii Fulco de Cham-paignelu* admitted.
1349. 1 Aug. William de Languterre on the presenta-tion of Simon Ministri Conventus de Mar-monstra.
1352. John Garny occurs.
1364. William Hlvet.

* This seems a " Fulk Paganell" in disguise.

1399. ⎫
1419. ⎬ John Wnell.

　　　　Priors of Tickford from the registers of Lincoln.

1419. Thomas Chace.

1431. John Carlisle, at whose death

1433. 10 Feb. Robert Blythe elected at his resignation.

1465. 18 June, Thomas Derneten.

1475. William Kirby occurs, but resigned 4 January.
　　　　William Pymberton admitted on the presen-
　　　　tation of the Convent at York; at his death in

1499. William Eynsham presented, 27 May, on his
　　　　resignation in

1501. 9 Nov., Thomas York presented, being made
　　　　Prior of St. Andrews, Northampton, 1503.
　　　　Thomas Brook, Prior of Snelshall, near
　　　　Whaldon, succeeded, and in

1523. Presided by York's resignation who had held an
　　　　inferior office in the house while Pymberton
　　　　was Prior.

Erection of　　The Parish Church was erected by one of the
the Church late Priors of Tickford; Browne Willis, who states
this fact, describes the Church as consisting of a
large and spacious nave, and two side aisles,
which are leaded, and chancel which is tiled;
the tower, which is at the West end, is coped at
top and covered with a rising roof, which is also
leaded, in the middle of which is a pole support-
ing a weathercock. It was designed for a spire,
and the scaffold holes yet remain round the tower, but the reformation coming on, the steeple
was never completed. In the second of Edward
VI. of pious memory, Mr. William Stokes, of
" Mulsoe." left the sum of twenty pounds for the

purpose of being " ymployed towardes the fynish- Church inge of Newport Steple, and the amendinge of ^{Steeple.} highewayes there," but it does not appear whether the directions in the will were complied with.

The entire disappearance of all remains of Some-rie's Castle has been accounted for on the suppo-sition that if the Church does not actually occupy a portion of the site on which the castle stood, it was partly erected with the materials; nor is the conjecture affected by the tradition that the stones for building the Church were dug from the stone pit on the Kickles farm, as it is probable additional materials would be required.

It will be in the recollection of some who may Church peruse these pages, that the architecture of the ^{Porch.} north porch prior to the extensive repairs in 1828, bore evident marks of a more ancient style than the rest of the fabric; and if on the decay of the Conventual Church, some portions of the ruined Castle were used in the erection of the Parish Church, (and certainly the marks of earth-works in the vicinity, and in the Church-yard itself, seem to bespeak that such might be the case) it is not surprising there should be no vestige of the Castle.

The Priory at Tickford was dissolved some 17 Henry few years previous to the general dissolution of ^{VIII.} the religious houses, and its suppression at this particular period, arose out of the following cir-cumstances : Pope Clement VII., granted Cardi-nal Wolsey, now in the meridian of his splendour, a legatine commission, to reform and suppress certain religious houses; an unusual concession, and as the sequel proved, a dangerous one to a needy Sovereign. Wolsey however is said to have acted conscientiously in the business, and devoted the revenues of the suppressed Monasteries to ecclesiastical purposes, particularly for the foundation of Colleges; in which, as both he and his master Henry asserted, "learned divines were to be reared and fostered, for the better combating the fast spreading heresies of that monster, Martin Luther." Tickford Abbey was amongst the number of Priories suppressed by Wolsey; and on the 24th January, the Prior, Thomas Brook, voluntarily resigned and surrendered his said Priory and his office of Prior into the hands of John, Bishop of Lincoln; and the Monastery became totally extinct and dissolved. Amongst the property surrendered, was "the Rectory and Parish Church, of which the King's progenitors had been immemorially patrons; and one of them had granted the same, to some former Prior of the Monastery, and the same had been appropriated by the said Prior and Monastery by confirmation of the King, by Letters Patent, and with the consent of the Ordinary the Bishop of Lincoln."

Tickford Abbey dissolved. A. D. 1525.

At the time of Brook's resignation, there were four resident and professed Monks on the establishment, who with their late Prior, departed from the house five days afterwards, (doubtless with Departure of the Monks. heavy hearts) leaving it without any Monk therein, whereby divine service could no longer be performed. It has been stated that the revenues of the Priory, which at its dissolution, were estimated at the annual value of £126. 17s. 5d., were appropriated towards the building of the Cardinal's two Colleges at Ipswich and Oxford ; but it appears that they were applied to the College at Oxford only.

The rank Tickford Priory held, can only be Its rank. known by a comparison with the revenues of other houses; and of the 645 in the kingdom, more than half their number were estimated below the annual sum of £200.

We have but little information respecting the Architectural structure. architectural structure of the Priory ; Browne Willis whose M.S. notes on this parish bear date 1735, speaks of the gateway and some other small remains of the Priory as standing within his time ; and says that within a few years there were to be seen five or six pillars which supported the nave of the Church, with the arches turned over them. In pulling down an old chimney some few years ago, there was discovered what was supposed to be a part of one of the windows of the original Chapel. The small pane of stained glass in the kitchen of the present Abbey, is said to be a relic of the old Priory.

There is a tradition, unsupported however by

authority, that Crawley Grange, the residence of
Mr. Boswell, was built by Wolsey, and that some
of its old carved furniture belonged to the Priory
at Tickford.

It is remarkable, that in the same year in which
the Cardinal suppressed so many Monasteries,
occurred his first misunderstanding with his
master, arising out of his conduct towards the
inmates of the suppressed Abbey at St. Albans;
and but two years afterwards, the sun of the
Cardinal's prosperity began sensibly to decline.

Scarcely had the broken hearted Wolsey been
consigned to the tomb in the Priory at Leicester,
when his Colleges were deprived of their revenues,
and Tickford Abbey, with its possessions, reverted to the crown; whereupon the King determined
to bestow them upon two Colleges (Queen's and
Christ Church) at Oxford; but for some unknown
reason, the property continued in the hands of the
crown, and the King endowed the Vicarage of
Newport with ten pounds per annum.

In the 33rd of the King's reign, a lease was
granted to Anthony Cave, of " All that Manor of
the late dissolved Priory at Tickford, together
with the whole site, circuit, and precinct, of the
same late priory." This gentleman resided at
Chicheley, and at his death, that estate passed
to the Chesters, through the marriage of his only
daughter with a member of that family.

In this same year, the lands and possessions of

the Priory were by a special Act of Parliament* Royal honor
annexed to the Manor of Ampthill, then created of Ampthill.
a Royal honor. The King being desirous of an-
nexing as many as possible of those Manors which
were in the neighbourhood, did not hesitate to
compel the Lords of several of them to exchange
lands with him. Sir John St. Leger was compelled to exchange the Manors of Newport Pagnell and Great Linford, for the Abbey possessions
of Cannonsleigh, in Devonshire; previous to this,
the Manors of Newport and Tickford had been
held by different Lords, but by this exchange
they both became the property of the crown. The
Duke of Bedford is the Lord of the Royal honor;
it has a Coroner of its own, and it is by the
authority of this Act of Parliament, that Mr.
Green of Woburn presides over those inquests
which are held in the hamlet of Tickford, that
portion of the Marsh End belonging to Tickford,
and nine other Manors in this county.†

Three years after the possessions of Tickford The general
Priory had passed into *lay* hands, the King's dissolution.
quarrel with the Pope, led to the entire destruc- A.D. 1537.
tion of the religious houses throughout the kingdom. Henry VIII. was in a much better position
to do this than Henry IV.; for having eased his

---

* 33 Henry VIII. Cap. 37.

† The Manors named in the Act, are "Molso, Great Lidforth, Little Lidforth, Stewkley, Little Brickhill, Bow
Brickhill, Wavingdon, North Crawley, and Swanburne."

shoulders of the galling papal yoke, he became
the temporal if not the spiritual head of the
Church, and one of his first acts in his new
capacity, was this suppression of the Monasteries;
a step, the boldness of which, we can in our day
have but little conception.   The judicious Camden has justly compared it to a torrent, which,
having thrown down the banks of ecclesiastical
authority, broke in upon the ecclesiastical state
of England, to the dismay of Europe.

All the houses whose yearly revenues did not
exceed two hundred pounds, were granted to the
King ; and in the next year, under the specious
pretence of rooting out superstition, the remaining houses were given up to the King's disposal;
he, as a master-stroke of policy, dividing the
Abbey lands and possessions amongst his courtiers
and dependants, and thus securing to himself the
future sanction of the Parliament, which was not
sitting at the time of the general dissolution. King's
commissioners were sent to every establishment,
when their finances underwent a rigorous scru-
tiny; a return being made of the Minister's accounts to the Court of Augmentation ; there was
however no return from Tickford, as the Abbey
had been virtually dissolved eight years before ;
so that our knowledge of its possessions is not so
complete as it would otherwise have been.

Most of the houses were in a short time every
where pulled down, a circumstance even then

greatly regretted by many, as the structure of some of them was exceedingly curious. How pathetically does Camden lament over the destruction of these memorials of the piety of our forefathers, built as he says they were, " to the honour of God, the propagation of the faith, good learning, and for the support of the poor ; but now, their revenues are squandered away, and the riches which had been consecrated to God by the pious munificence of the English, from the time they received Christianity, were in one moment dispersed, and if I may use the word without offence, profaned."

And yet perhaps the very fact of these possessions having passed into *lay* hands, was the great hinderance to the effectual re-establishment of popery in a subsequent reign ; for though Mary surrendered her share of these possessions, the example was lost upon her nobles ; so that while on the one hand, selfish principles became a bulwark against the power and authority of Rome, the fire and the rack was endearing to the great mass of the people, that Religion which could enable their victims to bear with fortitude and patience, such accumulated and inhuman sufferings.

Edward VI., to whom, through his inheritance of the crown, the Manor of Newport had descended, bestowed the Rectory, with all the tythes, both great and small, upon his youngest sister,

Survey of the Princess, afterwards Queen Elizabeth. As
the Manor. the Manor was surveyed during this year, it is
A. D. 1551.
likely that the bestowal of the gift was the occasion of it; and in the record of this survey, is the
first authentic information we have been able to
obtain respecting Bury Field: but the record
is silent as to the origin of the Common, treating
only of its extent and privileges.*

A. D. 1573.   On the 25th June, in the 15th year of Queen
Tickford
Park.   Elizabeth, a lease for twenty-one years was granted by Letters Patent, of the pannage in the woods
and underwoods in the park at Tickford, with the
herbage and pasture of the park, to George Annesley, Gentleman, and James, his son.   The
lease contained a reserved right of "sufficient

---

* From the Common being termed "Bury Field," it has
been supposed by some, that it acquired its name from
having been a place of interment, after some military engagement, or the ravage of some destructive plague. "Bury"
is a term of frequent use to describe the vill or seat of a
Nobleman; of which Astwood Bury, the site of one of the
finest old seats in this county, is an illustration; so that the
Common may have acquired its name from having been a
part of the domain annexed to the Castle. Others have
supposed that Bury has been derived from Beria, Berie,
Bery, Berry, signifying a large open field. That this term
describes a flat wide campaign, we have an instance in the
spacious meadow between Oxford and Ifley, which in the
reign of King Athelstan, was called Berry; and another in
the largest pasture at Quarrendon, in this county, which has
been let for £800. a year, and is to this day known as Bury
Field.

pasture for all and all manner of wild beasts, stags,
and deer, to the number of four hundred, being
in the park aforesaid, and which at all future
times shall be increased in the same park in
manner and form as they may conveniently be
sustained, by the view of the Surveyor of the
Manor of Newport Pagnell, for the time being."

The first member of the family of Annesley ^{Mr. Annes-}
who resided at Newport, was Robert Annesley, ^{ley.}
a younger brother of an ancient family in Nottinghamshire, which is said to have lived there
prior to the Conquest. Mr. Annesley was employed as bailiff or Steward in managing the
Abbey lands after the dissolution, and thus obtained a considerable share in those possessions.
In the list of Rectors of the Church of Great
Linford, it is stated that " Cristopher Daniel was
presented by Robert Annesley, of Newport Pagnell, on the 22nd of January, 1540." Mr. Annesley's will is dated 25th July, 1553, and
witnessed by the Vicar, William Hammond : he
describes himself as " Bailif of Newport," and
agreeably to his express desire was buried in the
Parish Church, but there is no monument remaining to his memory. Mr. George Annesley (who
obtained as his father's heir, the lease of Little
Linford, his two mills, and a house in Newport
Town which he had purchased ;*) married the
daughter of Robert Dove, of Molso, relict of

* The name of the house is given by Browne Willis, but

H

Mr. William Stokes, who left the twenty pounds for completing the steeple.

Lawrence Humphrey his birth. It was about this time, that Lawrence Humphrey was Dean of Winchester. He was born at Newport Pagnell in the year 1527, and was educated at Cambridge, from whence he removed to Magdalen College, Oxford, where he became Fellow, and received the appointment of Greek lecturer. The cruel persecution of Mary coming on, he left his cloistered retirement, and during her reign, resided abroad, as did many others; but on the accession of Elizabeth, returned to this country and was restored to his Fellowship. Two years afterwards he was chosen Professor of Divinity, and in the year following, was elected President of Magdalen College. He was made successively Dean of Gloucester and Winchester; and it is said, but for his puritanical principles, would, like his townsman Harley, have been advanced to His death. the dignity of the Episcopal Bench. He died in A. D. 1590. the year 1590, and has left as a memorial of his learning and piety, several classical works, together with a memoir of his contemporary, the celebrated Bishop Jewel.

Prior to this period, we have only met with two other persons, natives of Newport, who have risen to distinguished honors; Sir John

his M.S. is in some parts so illegible, as to be difficult, if not impossible to decipher.

Brokle, and Doctor Harley. In the 4th of Henry _{Sir John}
VI. [1424] Sir John Brokle was Sheriff of Lon- _{Brokle.}
don, and in 1434 he was Lord Mayor, Thomas
Chalton and John King, Sheriffs. Brokle must
have known the famous Sir Richard Whitting-
ton, he having been Lord Mayor six years
previous to Brokle's Shrievalty. The only information we have been able to obtain respect- _{Doctor}
ing Doctor Harley, is, that in the reign of Henry _{Harley.}
VII. [1504] he was Bishop of Hereford.

A short time before the expiration of Mr.
Annesley's lease of Tickford Park, the Queen by _{Tickford Park.}
her Letters Patent, on the 11th of November, _{A.D. 1592.}
granted the same in fee, to Thomas Compton,
Robert Wright, and Gelley Meyricke, Esquires,
" as well in consideration of the good, true, faithful,
and acceptable services to us, heretofore very
often done and performed by our very beloved
and faithful cousin, Robert, Earl of Essex, Knight _{Earl of}
of the most noble order of the Garter, and Mas- _{Essex.}
ter of our Horse, as for divers other good causes
and considerations us herewith especially moving,
and also on the humble petition of the said Earl;"
nine years after this proof of royal favor and
regard, a change came over the fortunes of the
man whom the Queen had delighted to honor;
on Ash Wednesday, the 25th February, in an _{A.D. 1601.}
inner court of the Tower, his head was severed
from his body. Tickford Park again reverted
to the Crown, and subsequently became by

Tickford Park.

purchase, the property of Sir John Fortescue, the Chancellor of the Queen's Exchequer.

The Priory

Doctor Adkins.

In the year 1600, Queen Elizabeth (in consideration of the sum of £1534. 6s.,) granted to Henry Adkins, Doctor of Physic, and Mary his wife, and the heirs of the said Henry for ever, the Rectory of Newport Pagnell, with the Manor or lordship of Tickford Priory, including the mansion house of the Manor or late Priory of Tickford, with the Manor of Caldecot, and all thereunto belonging. Dr. Adkins was one of the physicians in ordinary to the Queen, and was descended from the family of that name who had long resided at Clapham, in Surrey.

A. D. 1603.

Soon after the accession of James I., a conspiracy, or rather the project of one, was discovered, in which the owner of Tickford Park was in some measure implicated with the celebrated Sir Walter Raleigh; but even at the time of the discovery, Rapin states that it was the general opinion that the conspiracy was an arrant trick of the state to silence the most powerful opponents of the government.

A. D. 1604.

In the Parliament which assembled on the 23rd March, a long discussion arose on the subject of a double return for this county, Sir John Fortescue and Sir Francis Goodwin being alike claimants for the honor of the seat: the decision was in favor of Goodwin, but James being dissatisfied, and wishing the return of Fortescue, desired the house to re-consider their opinion. This plain interference with the established privileges of the house, would have led to serious 'consequences, but for the wisdom and moderation of Goodwin, who having resigned his seat, the county proceeded to a new election.

The gunpowder plot will long distinguish the third year of James's reign; in this dark deep tragedy, Sir Everard Digby of Gayhurst, played a fatal part. Sir Everard had but lately come into the possession of the estate at Gayhurst, by his marriage with Miss Mary Mulso, the heiress of the late proprietor. He contributed the sum of fifteen hundred pounds for the furtherance of the plot; the part assigned him was to accompany some others into Warwickshire, for the purpose of seizing upon the young Princess Elizabeth, as soon as they received intelligence of the success of their friends at Westminster. On the apprehension of Guido Fawkes, most of the conspirators fled by several ways to join their friends in the country; they were pursued from place to place, and soon after the discovery, Digby and several others were apprehended at a house belonging to one Stephen Littleton, at Holbeach, on the borders of Staffordshire.*

A. D. 1605.
Gunpowder plot.
Digby of Gayhurst.

Guido Fawkes.

* There is a local tradition, that Digby was for some time secreted in the chamber at Gayhurst house, called " Digby's hole." Rapin, whom we have followed in the text, does not state the precise time of Digby's arrest, but it was so

It is certainly most surprising, that a man of so mild and amiable a temper as Digby appears to have been, should have been so greatly led away by the intrigues of more designing men. While a prisoner in the Tower, he wrote with juice of lemon or otherwise, as opportunity offered ; and procured the conveyance of the letters to his lady, by such as had permission to visit him, and these papers were for many years preserved in the library at Gayhurst. Sir Everard Digby was put on his trial at Westminster, on the 27th of January following, and unlike the others arraigned with him, he pleaded guilty to the charge ; when sentence of death was passed upon him, he seemed to be very much affected, for making a low bow to those on the Bench, he said, " If I could hear any of your Lordships say you forgave me, I should go the more cheerfully to the gallows," to this all the Lords answered, " God forgive you, and we do." Three days afterwards, he was, with other conspirators, hanged, drawn, and quartered, at the west end of Saint Paul's, in London ; while at the scaffold, he asked forgiveness of God, the King, the Queen, the Prince, and

Digby's Trial.

A.D. 1606.

His execution.

quickly after the discovery of the plot, as to render it quite impossible for him to come to Gayhurst. It is true that Garnet and some others were concealed in a secret chamber at Henlip in Worcestershire, where after eight days search they were discovered ; and it is from this fact that the tradition at Gayhurst may have originated.

all the Parliament ; and protested, had he known
at first this act to have been so foul a treason,
he would not have concealed it to have gained a
world, requiring the people to witness that he
died penitent and sorrowful for it.

Anthony á Wood mentions a most extraordinary circumstance, as being at that time
generally known and believed ; that when the executioner plucked out Digby's heart, and according
to the accustomed usage, held it up saying, "Here
is the heart of a traitor," Sir Everard made
answer, " Thou lyest." He left two young sons, His sons.
afterwards Sir Kenelm, and Sir John, and ex-
pressed his great affection towards them by a
well written and pathetic paper, which he desired
might be communicated to them at a fit time, as
the last advice of their father. As the estate at
Gayhurst on the death of Sir Everard, did not
pass to the crown, it has been generally said that
before Digby had engaged in the conspiracy, he
artfully made over all his property to his infant
son ; but this appears improbable, as well from
his general character, as his dying confession.
The Encyclopædia Britannica, asserts that the
estates were forfeited, but afterwards restored ;
the more probable fact appears to be, that by the
marriage settlement the estate was secured to
the issue of the marriage.

Sir John Fortescue the owner of Tickford, died Sir John
Fortescue.
this year ; and it has been frequently stated, by A.D. 1607.

Bowen, amongst others, that he was "buried in the parish Church of Newport Pagnell, the learned Mr. Camden himself, directing the funeral as Clarencieux, King at Arms;" but this is incorrect, the Baronet was buried at Mursley, in this county, where was his family mansion, and which Elizabeth had visited, in one of her progresses.

Queen Anne.

The King having bestowed the Manors of Newport and Tickford upon his Queen Consort, the Lady Anne of Denmark, as a part of her jointure, the Manor of Newport was again surveyed, taken on the oath of twenty tenants of the Manor, and subscribed by them. The survey contains the names of all the tenants, (amongst others that of James Annesley, Gentleman) the respective state held by each tenant, the tenures of the ancient and improved rents, and the extent and boundary of the Manor.

St. John's Hospital.

Towards the end of the reign of Queen Elizabeth, the revenues of St. John's hospital became insufficient for the purposes for which they had been appropriated by the founder; the building itself, and the Chapel* wherein divine service was wont to be had and celebrated, being in a state of ruin and decay. On the accession of James, the state of the endowment appears to have been laid before him in a petition addressed

* In an Inquisition taken at Aylesbury, 20th September, 1598, it is stated "that part of the Chapell is decayed and pulled downe, by Thomas Annesley, gent."

to the crown, signed by Doctor Adkins, and The hospi-
tal. other inhabitants of the town.

King James on the 29th of June, granted a A.D.1616. Charter for the purpose of re-establishing the Charity in a somewhat different form; and the Queen, as the Lady of the Manor, graciously condescended to afford the Hospital her royal patronage. The Charter names a certain place and close for the site of the said Hospital, appoints one master who should be the Vicar of the parish for the time being, four governors, and six poor people, three men and three women: it declares that the foundation shall be called " the Hospital Queen of Queen Anne" in the village of Newport Pag- Anne's
hospital. nell, otherwise Pannell, in the county of Buckingham; grants a common seal, and constitutes the master and governors, a body corporate; appoints the Vicar, the Reverend Thomas Webb, to the office of master, and Doctor Adkins, James Annesley (High Constable) Matthias Conye, Gent., and Walter Hall, Yeoman, governors; and nominates William Dobbs, Robert Pearse, Thomas Rider, Alice Rider, Anne Whetstone, and Margaret Ives, as the first six inmates of the Hospital. The property belonging to the Charity is described at length, and in the course of this description, Newport Pagnell is once called a Borough.*

*Village, Town, and Borough, being each indiscriminately used in this Charter, seems to imply, that *Borough*,

A. D. 1619.
Remark-
able relic.

During this year, there was discovered within the parish Church a most remarkable relic of antiquity, the following particulars of which we find in Weever's funeral monuments: "In the north aisle of the Church, was found the body of a man whole and perfect, laid downe, or rather leaning downe, north and south; all the concavous parts of his body and the hollownesse of every bone, as well ribs as other, were filled up with solid lead. The skull with the lead in it doth weigh thirty pounds and six ounces, which, with the neck bone and some other bones in like manner full of lead, are reserved and kept in a little chest of the said Church, neare to the place where the corps were found, there to be showne to strangers as relics of admiration; the rest of all the parts of his body are taken away by gen-

in its ancient signification, meant a "Market Town," in which sense we apprehend "Lathburiensis," uses it in the Gentleman's Magazine, when he states, that at the Conquest, Newport was the only Borough in the county, the town of Buckingham being excepted. Mr. Hutchinson, the historian of Northumberland, supposes "Borough" was originally used to denote any kind of eminence, and might mean a fort or Castle, and that it is probably derived from the word describing the underground lodging of animals; and he gives it as his opinion, that when the term was first applied to human habitations, it signified the very same, for our original Boroughs in their primitive simplicity, were but so many human warrens, consisting of a set of underground caverns.

tlemen neare dwellers, or such as take delight in rare antiquities—this I saw."

The antiquary Cole, informs us that in the year 1776, the head was preserved in the library of St. John's College, Cambridge.

It is not known whether any other fragments of this relic are still in existence: we make no doubt says Lathburiensis, that the Rector of Great Linford, Doctor Napier, "a neare dweller, and one who took great delight in rare antiquities," was one of the depredators. But little is known of the nature of this extraordinary relic;* from the position as described by Weever, it has been conjectured, that the body was buried there, before, or at least very soon after the introduction of christianity into Great Britain.

* We have met with only three other instances of skeletons being found filled with lead: at Axminster, Devonshire; Gravesend, Kent; and Bradwell Ash, Suffolk. It has been supposed that the hollow of the bones has been thus filled with lead, from the melting of the leaden coffins occasioned either from lightning or some subterraneous vapours taking fire in the vault; or, as was the case at Gravesend, where they became so when the Church, being consumed by fire, the melted lead ran in all parts amongst the ruins, and entered many of the graves and vaults. Dr. Hunter who examined the bones found in the chancel of Bradwell Ash, gave it as his opinion that it was a method sometimes used to preserve relics. An account was given to the public in 1783, by Mr. Worth of Diss, of the bones found in Bradwell Ash, in which pamphlet a reference is made to the bones found at Newport Pagnell.

While digging for the foundation of Mr. Joseph Redden's house, there was found a skeleton laid in the trunk of a tree, which seemed to have been hewn hollow for that purpose, and had doubtless been interred in that spot soon after the mode of burying in wood was introduced. Several other skeletons which have been dug up northward of the Church, lead to the opinion, that the Church yard must once have extended in that direction; and the discovery of the skeletons referred to, has suggested the idea, that the parish Church was in existence on this immediate spot, prior to the erection of the Conventual Church in the time of William II., an opinion which deserves consideration; while on the other hand, some have supposed that interments took place within the fortifications of the Castle, and that the leaded skeleton was the corpse of some feudal chief.

Supposed antiquity of the Church.

Queen Anne dying in November, the Manor of Newport became the property of Prince Charles; and in the following year Doctor Adkins, for the sum of £4500., purchased Tickford Park of Lady Alice, widow of Sir John Fortescue.

A. D. 1620.

Mr. Francis Annesley who had already been advanced to the honor of Knighthood, and a Baronetcy, was in the year 1621, created Baron Mountnorris, and Viscount Valentia, Irish honors. Mr. Annesley was the first of his family who became ennobled, though some of his ancestors had been created Knights.

The Annesleys ennobled.

In the 21st year of his reign, King James made A. D. 1624.
an extensive grant of property in this parish to Doctor Adkins.
our townsman, Doctor Adkins, by the name and
description of Henry Adkins, Doctor in physic,
and one of the physicians in ordinary. The
Doctor was the favourite physician of the Court
during the reigns of Elizabeth and James, but
more particularly of the latter, whose eldest son,
Prince Henry, the Doctor on one occasion had
been the means of restoring to health.*

The King offered Adkins a Baronet's patent, The King's liberality to him.
which for some reason he declined; when, as a
reward for his professional services, his Majesty
made this extensive grant; two separate sums
are named in the deed of conveyance, but as
together they only amount to £250., it would
appear that they were merely fees paid to the
respective officers of the Court. The instrument
having described at length the property which
had passed by the grant of 1600, proceeds to
enumerate that which passed under this extended
grant, and it consisted of all those closes of land,
meadow, and pasture, in Newport Pagnell and
Lathbury, being late parcels or reputed parcels
of the Manor of Newport, namely: Bury close,

---

* Prince Henry however did not survive his father; the
eventful life of his younger brother Charles, seems to have
eclipsed the mild virtues of this amiable Prince. His well
known saying, that "all the pleasure in the world is not
worth an oath," ought never to be forgotten.

Bury field, Bury meadow, the Kickles' farm, and others ; all of which possessions were to be held in as full and ample a manner as any former possessor ever held the same, and as they came to the Crown by reason of the dissolution of any Monastery, or by pretext of any act or acts of parliament.*

A. D. 1627.
Newport
Manor.

King Charles I., on the 25th June, in the third year of his reign, in consideration of the sum of £343. 10s. 10d., paid by Sir Francis Annesley, and £837. 13s. 4d. paid by him, Roger Nichols, John Parker and John Chibnal, granted to Sir Francis " all that our Manor of Newport *Pannell*, in our county of Bucks., with all its rights, members, and appertenances, with the tolls and profits of the fairs and market in Newport, and all that tenement in Newport called Blackhouse, and the fisheries in our rivers."

Doctor
Napier.

It was at this time, that the celebrated Doctor Richard Napier, renowned as a famous physician of both body and soul, was Rector of the adjoining parish of Great Linford. In addition to the duties imposed on him by his Cure, he practised physic, and gave all the profits to the poor ; he was considered by his parishioners a man of exemplary piety and charity; but not content with these

* Many of our meadows and fields, still retain the same names by which they are described in this grant, we may instance " the shoulder of mutton," a portion of the meadow lying on the west side of the north bridge.

two-fold duties, he studied astrology, and imagining that he was assisted by the angel Raphael, answered in a wonderful manner all questions put to him. He once enquired of the angel which were the more in number, the good or evil spirits, and relates in his papers that he received for answer, " the good." He told Doctor Prideaux, in the year 1621, that in twenty years hence he would become a Bishop; and just twenty years afterwards, he was elevated to the See of Worcester. Doctor Napier foretold his His death. own death to the very day and hour, which happened while he was praying on his knees, which it is said had become horny* from his very frequent observance of that solemn duty; he died on the first of April, 1634, and was buried in the Church of Great Linford, without any memorial.

We now arrive at the eve of the " Grand Rebel- Grand rebellion. lion," during which period Newport Pagnell bore its share in the memorable events of that period. On the King's first misunderstanding with his parliament, and after its dissolution, he attempted to carry on the government by means of loans and benevolences, which he succeeded in obtaining by letters under the Privy Seal. One of these requisitions is in the manuscript collection

* Henry of Huntingdon relates a similar fact of Agatha, a daughter of William I.

of his Grace the Duke of Buckingham, in the library at Stowe, and is addressed to Sir William Andrewes of Lathbury, then a tenant of the illustrious John Hampden, who had property in that village, and owned one of its two Manors. The letter requires the loan of twenty pounds "for divers publique services, which, without manifold inconvenience to us and our kingdom, cannot be deferred;" the money was advanced, but it does not appear that it ever was repaid. It is said that a similar application was made to Sir John

Tyringham, who from his known steady adherence to his Sovereign, would doubtless readily accede to his Majesty's request.

It may be proper here to state, that the Andrewes of Lathbury, it is presumed, though not positively stated, descended from Sir Robert Andrewes, Knight, of Normandy, who came over with the Norman invader, and settled at Winwick, in Northamptonshire. Sir William, who is supposed to have received the honor of Knighthood from Queen Elizabeth, is the first of the family who is known to have resided at Lathbury. He resided there as early as 1596, and in 1599 became by purchase the Lord of one of the Manors in that village; but as Browne Willis writing about 1730, says the Andrewes are supposed to have resided at Lathbury 300 years, it has been conjectured that the family lived there for a long time previous to 1596.

In the year 1604, Sir William built the late Lathbury
mansion. mansion house* at Lathbury, causing to be affixed over the doorway, the following inscription :

Nec glis sit servus nec hospes hirudo.†

On the erection of the present edifice, Mr. Mansell had the inscription preserved, and it is now placed over the kitchen door.

* Sir Egerton Bridges styles it " a respectable looking old mansion." Topographer, 1790, Vol. 1.

In digging for the foundation of Mr. Mansell's new house, above thirty skeletons, apparently of females, were found covered with rough stones. Lysons, Bucks. page 693.

† *Let not your servant be a dormouse, nor your guest a horse leech.*

The following translation has been supplied by a clergyman of Northampton :

" Let not the hungry slave like dormouse rest,
Nor keep the griping leech in shape of guest."

Hirundo "a swallow," has been proposed as an emendation, and it certainly appears more in character with the hospitality of that day, to hope that the guest whould not fly away like a swallow, than to express a wish he might not prove a horse leech. It has been suggested whether the ancient mode of writing the word " *hirūdo*" does not favor the conjecture, the line above the u having been omitted by accident, or obliterated by time.

Such inscriptions were not uncommon in those days; the house of Mr. George Pike at Chicheley, built about the year 1600, originally known as Maunsell's farm, has this motto, " Piè, Justè, Sobriè," (Piously, Justly, Soberly); and over the doorway of an ancient house at Wymondham, Norfolk, is an inscription similar to the one at Lathbury.

On the decease of Sir William Andrewes in 1625, he was succeeded by his son William, who married Anne, the daughter of Sir Thomas Temple, of Stowe, by his wife the celebrated lady Hester Temple, who lived to see seven hundred descendants. In the year 1630, Sir William Andrewes served the office of Sheriff for this county.

Adkins of Tickford.

Doctor Adkins dying in this year, his estates descended to his son, who had been created a Knight and Baronet; he survived his father four years, and was succeeded by his son, Sir Richard Adkins. In the inquisition, post mortem, held before eighteen good and lawful men, it was declared that the tenure by which Sir Henry and his father held the Lordship or Manor of Tickford, with the mansion house of the said Manor or late Priory, the mill at Caldecot, the two grain mills, and the Rectory of Newport Pagnell, was of the Lord the now King, as of his manor of Hampton Court, by Knight service by the twentieth part of one Knight's fee, and were worth by the year five pounds; and that the estates within the Lordship of Newport Pagnell, including the park of Tickford, were held of the Lord the King, as of his honor of East Greenwich, and were worth by the year ten pounds; and the jury further declared, that they were ignorant, of whom or by what service Sir Henry or his father held the other parts of their property, which were situated in this parish.*

The Honorable Arthur Annesley granted to Annesley. Mr. James Annesley a tanner, residing in Marsh End, a lease of the fulling mill holme, now called Annesley holme. The mill which was on the stream of the Lovatt, was doubtless one of the two mills mentioned in Domesday, and there are still some remains of it in existence.

It was during this year the town first began A.D. 1643. to experience the effects of civil war. Bedford Sir Lewis had been just taken by Prince Rupert; Sir Lewis Dives. Dives, of Bromham hall, was at the head of the King's interest there; and he having made himself somewhat obnoxious to the parliament, Sir Sir Samuel Samuel Luke was ordered to apprehend him, but Luke. in this attempt he was not only unsuccessful, but received four wounds, Dives saving his life by swimming the Ouze, near Bromham; Luke's soldiers however were amply rewarded by the plunder of Bromham hall. The King now held his Court at Oxford, from whence orders were

* Knight's service was a remnant of the feudal tenures, and was one of those fictions of law which supposed all the land in the kingdom to be held of the King. By this tenure, the tenant was bound to perform a service in war unto the King, or the mesne Lord of whom he held by that tenure. In the time of William I., there were sixty thousand two hundred and fifteen Knight's fees, whereof twenty-eight thousand and fifteen, were in the possession of the religious houses.

issued to Sir Lewis Dives, Sir John Digby of
Gayhurst, (son of the ill-fated Sir Everard) and
Colonel Urrey, who had lately revolted from the
parliament, to take Olney, and afterwards to seize
upon Newport Pagnell, where it was proposed to
establish a garrison of fifteen hundred men.   In
obedience to these orders, Sir Lewis Dives having
possessed himself of Newport, threw up the embankment in Bury Field and Marsh End, and
surrounded that part of the town then called
Back Lane, with a stone wall; he issued orders
for bringing in provision, and compelled the inhabitants to work at the fortifications, designing
to establish a barrier between Bristol and Peter-
borough, and so cut off supplies from the metropolis.   The adverse party thus describe the progress of the works: "Several cavaliers came
into Bedfordshire, which county they have woe-
fully plundered ; they have seized upon the towne
of Newport Pannell, in the upper part of Buckinghamshire, which lyeth between Bedford and
Stoney Stretford ; and have forced the inhabitants
thereabouts to come in and entrench it, and they
are drawing the water about it the better to
strengthen and fortifie it, their drift being to
intercept all cattell and other provisions that
shall come out of the adjoining counties to London, hoping thereby to cut off all victuall from
this city [London] and so to starve it, if they be

Newport taken by the Cavaliers.

30th October, 1643.

not timely prevented and unnestled out of that place."

Four days later, the Welsh Mercury has the following curious article in reference to the same subject: "We heare from Newport Pagnell, in Buckinghamshire, that the cavaliers make creat fortifications to keep awle her cood cattles and Welsh runts and other provisions, from coming to London, and by keeping out the fat beasts, was make her have a verie leane citie; if her should stop all passages, yet some of her sheeses have a creat many leg (her will not say maggots) that will in despite of the cavaliers, carrie them up to London, with superscriptions upon them to deliver them to her cousen sheese monger."

Though so much importance seems to have been attached to the possession of Newport Pagnell, as being the means of cutting off supplies from the metropolis, the main road from London to Northampton passed through Stony Stratford, at which place it will be remembered, the body of Queen Eleanor rested in its journey to the tomb, and where at a later period, the young King Edward was arrested. The road through Newport appears to have been used on some occasions, as in the year 1575, when Elizabeth passed by this way, in one of her progresses. In feudal times, the Castle must have been an insuperable barrier to any but privileged parties passing through Newport;

The ancient road.

and at this time, it is probable that the road passed over the Woad meadow, and crossing the river at a washway, passed near the Abbey in a track of which there are still evident traces. On the destruction of the Castle, a road seems to have been cut through the hill on which it stood, and it is supposed that the old public road passed through the cutting and by the river, an opinion corroborated by the fact, that a large portion of the High street is private property. Which ever may have been the original road, it is certain, that while an hostile force had pos-

Civil war, session of Newport, the enemy must suffer much inconvenience, and this seems all that Dives could hope to effect when he established a garrison here. Dives in an eminent degree possessed the confidence of his party, and his seasonable presence was of great service to the royalists of this, and his native county ; of his movements as governor of the garrison, we are only informed that he retaliated the plunder of Bromham hall, upon his enemy's house at Hawnes, near Bedford, and apprehended some committee-men at Ampthill.

The parliament promptly adopted measures to rescue Newport Pagnell from the enemies' hands; "a towne," which, according to Needham, was "geometrically situated for the defence of the

associated counties,* and Essex, Skippon, Luke, _{A.D. 1643.}
Harvey, and Wilson, were commissioned to dis-
possess the royalists, and establish themselves in
their place.   Essex marched with his soldiers
from Windsor, where he had been resting since
the battle at Newbury on the 30th of September,
and came to St. Alban's, when a gallant regiment of the city, under the command of Colonel Colonel
Wilson joined him, and detachments were sent ^{Wilson.}
from that and other regiments to this place.†
On Monday, the 30th of October, the army halted
at Dunstable, and on Saturday marched to New- Newport
port by way of Brickhill, thus making their ap- taken by
proach on the least defensive position; the bridge Essex.
at Tickford offering a serious obstacle to an
attack in that direction.   Though the army ob-

* Bucks was one of the first counties which joined in an
association for mutual defence on the side of the parliament.

† Essex and Skippon are well known characters of that
day; and Wilson we are informed, was the only son of his
wealthy father, heir to a large estate in land of two thousand
per annum, and partner with his father in a great personal
estate employed in merchandise; but he nevertheless held
himself obliged to undertake the journey, as persuaded that
the honor and service of God, the flourishing of the gospel
of Christ, and the true protestant religion, might in some
measure be promoted by this service; and that his example
in the City of undergoing it, might be a means the more to
persuade others not to decline it.   Upon these grounds, he
cheerfully marched forth with a gallant regiment of the
City, called the Orange regiment.   *Whitelock's Memorials.*

Dives'
retreat.

tained possession that same [Saturday] evening, it does not appear that this was done without encountering some resistance. Lord Clarendon states, that " Sir Lewis Dives, through a mistake of orders received from Oxford, drew off his forces, when the enemy possessed themselves of Newport Pagnell and made it a very useful garrison ;" though some have thought this improbable, as being inconsistent with Dives's general character. It is probable that Sir Lewis was ignorant of the near approach of aid, for Lord Biron had ad-advanced as far as Broughton, but ascertaining the altered position of affairs, immediately returned. It is certain that Dives did not neglect his trust, and while fortifying the town, encouraged his soldiers by reports of a disaffection amongst the trained bands, but finding his resources unequal to the contest, he abandoned the town and

Earl of
Essex.

joined the King at Oxford. Essex took prompt and decisive measures for securing the possession of the town ; the fortifications commenced by Dives, were strengthened and increased, and on the 15th of November, Kingdome's Weekly Post reports, that " Our Post bringeth intelligence from Newport Pagnell, that Sargeant Major Skip-

Major
Skippon.

pon is made master of the works there, and that the carpenters and the pavioners are fortifying the towne very strongly ; that as the water doth compass the towne as it were on two sides of it, so trenches from the said moate are digged with drawbridges and sluices, to be completed Fortifica- according to the Sergeant Major's directions ; all tions. which goeth forward very fast."* Agreeably to the spirit of the times " His Excellency enjoined strict discipline, and constant prayer."

While Skippon was superintending these works, the Earl of Essex was occupied in a series of Earl of engagements at Towcester, Stony Stratford, Al- Essex. derton, and Olney, in all of which he was victorious ; his last engagement was immediately before the fortifications of Newport, in which he repulsed a party of royalists commanded by the gallant Sir Charles Lucas.

On the 11th of December, the House of Com- The Garri- mons voted the sum of one thousand pounds per son. A.D. 1643. month, for the due maintenance of the garrison at Newport ; and a few days after, Essex gave up the command, when it devolved upon Skippon, Major Skip- who, instead of quietly resting in his winter quar- pon. ters, was ever on the alert in the service of his party. Having obtained intelligence that Grafton Attack on house was fortified by the royalists, thus "leaving Grafton house. open the rode which did much mischief to the city of London, he at once undertook to bring it in obedience to the Parliament, and which service

* From the description here given, it would appear that the embankment near the Gas works, lately levelled, formed a part of the fortifications, and that the trench, with the drawbridges and sluices, passed over the garden ground now occupied by Mrs. Nichols, and extended to the earthworks in Bury Field.

L

he did most gallantly performe ;" of this engagement, we have the following interesting particulars in a pamphlet published a few days after the
event :* " On Thursday night, the 21st of December, about eight o'clocke, there was a command given for a thousand foot or thereabouts,
to be ready to march the next morning by two
o'clocke ; whereupon the soldiers assembled at
Lathbury. the rendevouse at Lathbury, where a brave party
of horse met with Colonel Norwich's troop, with
four pieces of artillery, and proceeded on their
march to attack the strong house held by the
Lady Crane, at Grafton Regis, and they soon after
met with a party of horse and foot which had
come from Northampton to their assistance.
When they came within sight of the house, the
old soldiers of Lord Manchester, (those from
Northampton) out marcht the troops from Newport, and gave the onset on the house very
courageously, and were as bravely answered;
but by reason of the strength of the walls, and
well fortifying of the same, the musquiteers did
them small injury at that time ; and though they
planted two field-pieces against the house, and
played upon it smartly, yet the beseiged successfully withstood the attack. On Saturday, the
Newport troops relieved my Lord's soldiers, and

* Published at length in Mr. Baker's valuable History
of Northamptonshire.

when any advantage could be gained against the loyalists, it was made use of. The beseiged had very long pieces and could reach their enemies at a great distance; at length with difficulty some of Skippon's men planted a piece against the weakest part of the house, and before evening, had beaten down the breast-work on the top of the house which had done great annoyance, as also a window out of which the beseiged had shot at the troops. On the following morning, the Orange regiments were relieved by the Northampton forces, and about two hours after Colonel Wellam had the guard, they within sounded a parley; but through the eagerness of the soldiers the drummer was shot, but not slain outright, whereupon they sent out a trumpeter, and had parley granted for two successive half hours, after which, the beseiged yielded themselves prisoners, being in number nine score and seven, besides officers; Sir John Digby of Gayhurst, as chief, signed the capitulation, there was an officer of note named Major Brookbank, Captain and Lieutenant Longueville,* with divers Captains, some of whom were worth £700. per annum; eighty troopers, all with swords, pistols, and carbines, several foot prisoners; Henry Ratliffe, an Ensign, Archdeacon Beeley, Parson Crompton, Parson Bunning (who according to Walker was a learned young man, a very good preacher of good life and deserts,)

Grafton house.

Sir John Digby.

Longue-villes.

* Probably of Wolverton.

Grafton house.

and one hundred foot, armed with muskets. About two o'clock the troops entered the house, where they found great and rich plunder, which they had for their paines. In this attack, the troops from the garrison at Newport lost about twenty men, ten were wounded, and nine others were hurt by the explosion of their own powder.

On the following morning (Christmas day,) orders were given to fire the huts which had been erected in the field; and partly out of revenge, and partly for the prevention of future inconvenience, the house itself was destroyed by fire. The Orange and Green regiments assisted by the forces from Northampton, conducted the prisoners besides several gentlemen who came voluntarily to the garrison, but the foulnesse of the weather, and the deepnesse of the way, coupled with the fatigue all had undergone, rendered their march very labourious." Sir John Digby

Sir John Digby committed to the Tower.

was escorted from Newport and committed to the Tower; on obtaining his liberty, he rejoined the royal army, and was subsequently killed in one of the engagements of that day. A few days after this campaign, the trained bands quitted the garrison, (the command of which devolved upon Sir Samuel Luke,) they returned to London, and

A. D. 1644.

on the nineteenth of January, assembled in Cornhill, publicly to offer their thanks to Almighty God for their safe return.

Sir Samuel Luke was appointed governor of the

garrison, and it is said resided at the house on the Sir S. Luke
Green, now occupied by Mrs. Levi; he probably governor.
remained at Newport from the time of his arrival
in November, for he accompanied Skippon with
the men under his command, in the attack on
Grafton house. As a reference to Sir Samuel His person-
Luke's personal history, may serve to illustrate al history.
his character, we subjoin the following particulars: he was descended from a respectable
family at Cople, near Bedford, and his mother
was a daughter of Sir Valentine Knightley,
whose descendants still reside at Fawsley in
Northamptonshire. Sir Samuel was deformed
and dwarfish, but these physical defects were
amply compensated by superior mental endowments; Josiah Ricraft calls him " the valiant
victorious Sir Samuel, who was never knowne to
turne his backe upon the enemy; he was a true
hearted publike engaged covenant keeping and
virtuous true hearted English Knight, to whom
England may be indebted, and he not indebted
to England."

Luke was knighted by James I., and sat for
the town of Bedford in the long parliament. He
had early the command of a regiment which he
raised, and displayed a magnificent ensign embla-
zoned with the symbols of religion and liberty,
these being the favourite professions of his party.
An intercepted warrant (which appears in one of
those scarce pamphlets published at this period,

Sir S. Luke's regiment.

and now preserved in the British Museum) will serve to show by what means Sir Samuel Luke raised his regiment; it is addressed to the constable and inhabitants of Salford, and signed by Thomas Pots of Toddington, on the first of July, 1643.— " These are to signifie that it is Sir Samuel Luke's desire that it be published in your parish with all speed, that he will no longer dally with, or by more fair wayes and meanes claw his countrymen, seeing that it is altogether vain and fruitless, but he is resolved that if all persons in every parish between sixteen and sixty, being able to carry

Leighton Buzzard.

armes, shall not severally appear at Leighton on Monday morning next, by seven of the clock, with all provisions with them, and armes, and weapons, for the service of the state and their own safety, he will proceed against such cold and insensible persons and parishes of this county with that rigour and severitie as is done in other places, that the good may not remaine always scoft and derided at, but that they may receive such ease and comfort by such his proceedings, as is agreeable to all manner of equitie and good conscience ; and to let them know that all such as do come are to march away presently, and therefore desire them to come provided for that purpose ; fayle you not hereof, and to bring a list of the names of every man, at your peril."

The governor's activity.

We find Sir Samuel Luke very active in his duties as governor of the garrison at Newport ;

he was successful in storming a house at Hilles-
don, but nearer home he had not the same good
fortune, for the Earl of Cleveland succeeded in
maintaining a station at Stony Stratford, and on
one occasion the Newport soldiers suffered a defeat
within sight of their own garrison ; it is stated
that a party of the royalists from Stratford made
a sudden attack on the governor's house with a The royal-
design of carrying him off as their prisoner, but ists attack
in this attempt were defeated, as Sir Samuel his house.
succeeded in defending himself in one of the
rooms of his house, until the soldiers of the garrison to whom the alarm had been given, came
to his assistance ; and it appears that on the 21st
of March, 1644, the House of Commons "ordered,
that Sir Samuel Luke be directed to strengthen
the fortifications in the town of Newport Pagnell."

Acting under these instructions, the governor
added to the fortifications, and erected several Erection of
ill-looking barracks in the market-place ; but as Barracks.
they obstructed the thoroughfare, they were subsequently taken down.

In those days as in the present, money was the
sinews of war ; and it must be admitted that the
parliament resorted to many unjustifiable and
indeed unconstitutional means of supplying their
necessities ; a copy of a warrant issued by Sir Warrant to
Samuel Luke for pillaging the royalists of this pillage the
royalists.
neighbourhood, affords a striking proof of the arbitrary mode of proceeding, and while it throws

some light upon Luke's official transactions, affords at the same time much valuable information, respecting this town and its vicinity.

"By vertue of a warrant from the Committee for sequestration of estates of delinquents and papists, to me directed, these are to will and require you to present warning to all tenants, bailifs, and officers of all delinquents and papists within your parish, particularly hereafter named, to bring in all their rents to the Committee at Newport at the Sarazen's head, upon the 25th day of this instant, April, by nine of the clock of the morning, to be paid for the use of the King and the kingdome; requiring you to warn two or three able men in your parish to appear before the said Committee at the place and time appointed, to do such further service as they shall be required unto. And yourselves, there as you and they will answer it at your peril; dated the 17th day of April, 1644. All rents due to any Bishops, Deans, Chapters, and Prebends, or any rents due to any College or Hall in Oxford or Cambridge."

Saracen's head Inn, 1644.

Though the list of delinquents and papists as printed in the diurnals, is extremely incorrect, there is with one or two exceptions, but little difficulty in adding thereto, the residence of the parties. The Earl of Northampton, Castle Ashby; Sir Robert Throckmorten, Weston Underwood; Sir John Digby, and the Ladie Digby,

Gayhurst; Sir John Tyringham, Tyringham; The Roy-
Sir Thomas Dayrell, Lillingstone Dayrell; the alists.
Lady Farmar, Easton Neston; Spencer Lucy,
Esq., Haversham; Thomas Longfield, Esq., [query
Longueville, of Bradwell ;] Mr. James Digby,
Dr. Nevill, Dr. Giles, king's physician, Dr. Dillon
of Shenly, Mr. Coates, Mr. Roger Hacket, North
Crawley, Mr John Crome, [query *Crane of
Loughton*]; Mr. Stiles, Edward Bolsworth [query
Leighton Buzzard]; to this list of royalists in the
neighbourhood we may add the names of Sir
Anthony Chester, of Chicheley; Sir Kenelm
Digby, of Gayhurst; Napier, of Great Linford; Foster, Slingsby, Hillersden, Lane, and
Willoughby. It may not be uninteresting to
subjoin the names of the following gentlemen
who adhered to the parliament: Andrewes,
Temple, of Stanton Barry, Lane, Tyrrell, Duncombe, and Rawlins. We have not been able Compound
to ascertain how far Sir Samuel Luke proceeded in for their
compelling the royalists to compound for their Estates.
estates; that they often did we shall have frequent occasion to observe, and it would appear
that all the royalists residing in this neighbourhood, were forced to compound; we learn from
other sources that the estates of Sir Anthony
Chester of Chicheley were sequestered, and
that the soldiers of this garrison did considerable injury to his mansion.

M

Sir Lewis Dives compounded for his estates for the sum of £184. 17s. 6d., and Thomas Longueville, of Bradwell, Bucks., Esq., for the sum of £520.

Sir Kenelm Digby

Sir Kenelm Digby was perhaps one of the most devoted royalists in this neighbourhood, and he is so distinguished a character, that we may advert somewhat slightly to him. He was born at Gayhurst in 1603, and was Knighted by James on which occasion if the Duke of Buckingham had not guided the King's hand instead of touching his shoulder, Digby says he had certainly run the point of the sword into his eye. Digby led a most active life, but neither the business of the Court, nor the bustle of the Camp could quench his love for learning, and his study of philosophy; he found out several useful medicines which he gave away freely to the people, and greatly distinguished himself by his sympathetic powder for the cure of wounds at a distance; his discourse on this subject made some noise in the world.*

* Sir Kenelm cultivated with great success the *helix pomatia*, the largest species of land snail in England. These snails are not indigenous, but naturalized in Britain, and have thriven so well in our climate as to be found now in some parts in great abundance.—One of the Arundel family dispersed them all over the downs and in the woods at Albury; his example was followed by others in different parts of the Kingdom, but by none with so much success

At the commencement of the civil wars, Sir Kenelm made great exertions in the King's cause, and the parliament caused him to be imprisoned in Winchester house, from which he was released in 1643; and after having compounded for his estates, he was ordered to leave the country, when he retired to France, and during his residence there, was of great service to the widow of his royal master. At the restoration, he returned to London and established in his house at Covent Garden, those literary assemblies to which he had been accustomed in France, and which he seems to have first introduced in this country; he died in 1665, and was buried in Christ Church within Newgate, where several years before his death he had erected a superb monument to the memory of his wife. On account of his early talents and great proficiency in learning, Sir Kenelm Digby was compared with the celebrated Pico dela Mirandola, who was declared to be one of the wonders of human nature; it has however been supposed that his learning was not so profound as it seemed to be, his acquirements being adorned with elocution and address,

as by Sir Kenelm Digby, who dispersed them about Gayhurst.—Rees' Cyclop.—There is a tradition that Sir Kenelm introduced them as an article of food for his Lady, for the cure of the consumptive malady, under which she laboured.—They are not now to be found in the grounds at Gayhurst.

caused his learning to appear to the best possible advantage. The gallant Knight knew how to shine in a circle of ladies, as well as amongst the literati of his day, and was as much attended to when he spoke on the most trifling, as when he discoursed on philosophical subjects.

A.D. 1644. In the month of May, Sir Samuel Luke sur-
Sir S. Luke prised Sir John Fortescue, at Islip in Northamptonshire, and succeeded in taking fifty pounds in money, fifty horses, and twenty-seven prisoners, Sir John Fortescue being one.

George Fox During this period there was for some months residing in this town, a man destined to occupy a large share of public attention; the celebrated George Fox, lodged at the sign of the Waggon and Horses, near the Cannon Corner, and records in his diary, that he left Newport "in the fourth month of 1644, then called June."

The King pursued. The King who had been at Aylesbury, passed through Stony Stratford to Woburn, where he reposed at Woburn house: on his departure in July, Brown and Waller pursued his Majesty with two hundred dragoons from this garrison, but were foiled, owing to the superiority of the King's cavaliers: it is to this fact Butler is supposed to allude, when he asks,

" Did not they swear at first to fight,
For the King's safety and his right?
And after march'd to find him out,
And charged him home with horse and foot? *

* Hudibras, Part II., p. 159.

From various notices in the diurnals, we learn The Garrison. that remittances to the garrison were irregular and inadequate to its demands; in July, complaints were made that the establishment was in great want of men and money, supplies not being sent in from the associated counties.

Supplies having been forthwith granted, several vigorous movements were made under Lydcote, Ennis, and Andrewes; Ennis breaking out into Oxfordshire, routed various parties at Islip, Bicester, and Kidlington; Lydcote was defeated at Abthorpe, and fell by the sword of the noble Earl of Northampton, who with his three brothers, had fought with great courage and bravery; and Captain Henry Andrewes of Lathbury, was found Captain Henry Andrewes. of great service to the garrison; the governor had given him a Captain's commission, with a promise of the first Majority that became vacant.

Mr. Andrewes' name occurs in a letter dated 28th October, 1644, from the governor, to Sir Oliver Luke, his father, requesting an order of parliament, to force the county to work, as done at Banbury, and to collect money as allowed at Aylesbury; this letter was signed by Captain Andrewes, and several others of Luke's friends. After the defeat of the parliament forces at Banbury, Mr. Andrewes was appointed to command a troop there; a letter of recommendation to Lord Say, states that he is " a gentleman of worth and honor," and requests that he may have " accommodation fit for a gentleman," and Luke elsewhere describes him as " a person of approved fidelity ;" he appears to have been heartily engaged in this business, for on presenting this letter to Lord Say, he requested additional stores for his troop, and obtained by means of petition, one hundred and sixty stand of arms from the committee.

Upon the occasion of Lord Say declining any further interference in these matters, Captain Andrewes spoke to his uncle, Sir Peter Temple, to procure for him saddles for his men. On the 1st of November, he addresses Sir Samuel Luke from the garrison at Newport, concerning his exertions and ill success; it would appear by this letter, that Mr. Andrewes had returned from Banbury, and presided over the garrison here, during the Governor's absence.

Sir S. Luke. The advance of the King's troops, rendered necessary Sir Samuel Luke's attendance at the garrison, and the House of Commons ordered him to proceed thither, which he did ·about the month of January, but we hear nothing of his movements further than that as Member for the town of Bedford, pursuant to the self-denying ordinance, he was preparing to resign the governorship of Newport Garrison.

A. D. 1645.
Captain
Andrewes.

In February 1645, Captain Andrewes was stationed with his own troop, and two companies of horse near Daventry, in order to lie near that

town and the royal army, until the return of
Colonel Lydcote. On the third of March, he
marched with some troopers to Horton, to recon-
noitre a party of the enemy's horse, and on return
to the garrison, brought with him four prisoners.

In the month of May, Captain Andrewes with
two troops consisting each of about sixty horse,
was dispatched to the relief of Gloucester. He
arrived at Warwick while that town was in the
possession of the enemy, and on the next day, a
detachment from the army of Prince Maurice
arrived within two miles of it. Colonel Brydges
drew out his own regiment of foot, with about
twenty horse to oppose them; in which he was
joined by Captain Andrewes at the head of the
Newport cavalry. The royalists being defeated,
a quantity of plunder which they had acquired,
fell into the hands of the victorious party.

At this time the long promised Majority became
vacant, and was given to one Ennis, then abroad,
notwithstanding the endeavours and frequent
letters of the governor in favor of Captain Andrewes. Mr. Andrewes soon after left the army,
and broke off his connection with this party,
probably disgusted at the treatment he had received; Sir Samuel Luke complains in one of
his letters, that Andrewes' friends will not believe
but that he had a hand in Ennis's promotion.

On the ninth of this month, the townsmen of
Newport Pagnell petitioned, that Mr. Cockayne

of Hatley might succeed Luke as the governor
of the garrison ; but on the King's advance, they
requested his continuance, and Sir Samuel's term
was accordingly prolonged.

While these events were transpiring in Newport, the King was active in his attempts to
maintain his royal authority; he had stormed
Leicester, and was now at the neighbouring
town of Daventry, for the purpose of bearing
upon the garrisons and fortresses in the eastern
associated counties; but instead of acting with
promptness and decision, the King's movements
were characterised by doubt and uncertainty;
and while he, perchance presuming upon "that
divinity which doth hedge a King," was trifling
away his time in the amusement of the chase,
and jading the spirits of his men by marches and
countermarches, his ever watchful enemies were
collecting their scattered forces, that they might
strike a blow which should decide the quarrel.

The Garrison   At this critical moment the garrison at Newport
was in so defenceless a state as justly to excite the
governor's alarm, this appears from the two following letters preserved by Rushworth, but he does
not state to whom they were addressed. " Sir,
This messenger will assure you that his Majesty is
at Harborough, and his march is intended either
for Northampton or this place, as the report goeth ;
therefore I beseech you let the foot belonging to
this garrison be sent home with all speed ; and

if you can spare us any more, they will be most The Garri-
acceptable, for we shall want above a thousand son.
men to man our works in any reasonable manner.
We want all provisions, and if we escape a storm
we cannot hold out long, therefore desire you to
consider him who is yours in all serviceable respects commendable, *Sam. Luke.* This 5th of
June, 1645, four o'clock in the morning. I beseech you Sir let the General be acquainted with
our condition." The other letter is as follows,
and was written one hour afterwards: " Gentlemen, The enemy lies this night at Harborough,
and all intelligence being that they intend for
this town, how ill we are provided you cannot
but know, our horse and men being commanded
away, and we are not six hundred foot left in the
town; I desire as you tender either your own or
our good, to haste hither what men you can, for
we have need of two thousand men to man the
works, they are so large, and at this time so
indefensible. This is all at present can be as-
sured you, from yours to serve you, *Sam. Luke.*"

Fortunately for Luke, the parliament anticipa-
ted his necessities, and while he was penning Sir Thomas Fairfax at
the despatches, Fairfax received orders to abandon Sherington.
the siege at Oxford, and march towards the King.
The general arrived here if not on the 7th, at
any rate on Sunday the 8th of June;* he rested

* Rapin states that he did not march from Oxford till
the 7th. Sir Thomas Fairfax we heard was this day come

N

at Sherington,† from which place he despatched letters to both houses requesting the assistance *Oliver Crom-* of Cromwell; he received the consent of the *well.* houses by a special messenger, and on the 11th, while quartered at Wootten, two miles from Northampton, Fairfax wrote to Cromwell enclosing the vote of the House of Commons. On *Battle of* Saturday, the 14th of June, the contending armies *Naseby.* met in a large fallow field near the town of Naseby. Cromwell having arrived on the previous evening, the parliamentary army were enabled to concentrate their forces; the men deeply imbued as they were with the religious enthusiasm of the times, having sung a psalm, sat down composedly with their arms in their hands, and waited for the attack. During the engagement, "the popular unflinching Skippon" who had for some time commanded the garrison in this place, was dangerously wounded in the side; *Sir Anthony* *Chester.* and amongst the royal army, Sir Anthony Chester of Chichely, highly distinguished himself by his bravery and courage.

to Newport Pagnell, so speedy he is beyond all expectation in his advance.—Perf. Diur June 2 to 8.—On the following day it is stated that Lieutenant General Cromwell with about 3,000 foot and 1,000 horse on Saturday marched towards Newport Pagnell.

† There is a tradition that the army encamped in the field before the Rectory House at Sherington, and but little doubt can be entertained that John Bunyan was amongst the number.

The King's indecision, coupled with the want of discipline in his army, led to a most signal defeat; his disasters inspired his enemies with courage, and they at once perceived they had struck the fatal blow, the city of London was so elated with the victory won at Naseby, that on the 17th, they feasted both Houses at Grocer's Hall; after dinner they sang the 46th psalm, and so parted.

Sir Samuel Luke was not in the train of the victorious army; he remained at the garrison, and with his usual vigilance, scoured the country in search of fugitives, whom on the 16th he forwarded to London; and on the 30th, his prolonged commission expired, when as stated by some he resigned the office of governor, and was succeeded by D'Oley, a native of Weston Turville, who held the office of Major General for Bucks., and one or two other counties. Sir S. Luke

There appears to have been some misunderstanding on the subject of the appointment to the office of governor of the garrison. Whitelock states that on the 9th of August, Mr. Brown had appointed Mr. Temple to the office; Sir Thomas Fairfax was dissatisfied with this arrangement, and he desired that Lieutenant Cockayne might receive the appointment; it seems probable that the dispute was decided by Sir Samuel Luke continuing, or at any rate being re-appointed to the command, as Browne Willis states that on Governor of the Garrison.

A.D. 1645. the 3rd of September, Luke presided here as governor, and the House voted the sum of eighty pounds per month, for the support of the garrison. This monthly payment was in addition to supplies received from other sources, as but a few days before, we find it recorded that Sir John Tyrrell's composition of £600. was approved, of which sum £500. was ordered for the garrison of New-port. About this time an act of parliament was passed for re-modeling the garrison.

The soldiers of the garrison here, alike with others, partook of the religious enthusiasm of the times; the officers and men amongst the round-heads got into the pulpits and preached as well as fought, they are described by Butler as being

> Free of every spiritual order,
> To preach and fight and pray and murder.

Cromwell himself preached, and there is still in existence a sermon entitled Cromwell's Learn-ed, Devout, and Conscientious Exercise, held in the town house, Lincoln's Inn Fields, of Sir Peter Temple, of Stanton Barry; and we have met with two Exercises preached in Newport Pagnell Paul Hobson. during this year, by Captain Paul Hobson. In the advertisement to the impartial readers, the Captain-parson thus complains of the treatment he received : " It is now about a year and a half since, for delivering of this following treatise in a quiet and peaceful manner in Newport Pagnell and Lathbury, in the county of Buckinghamshire,

I was imprisoned by the governor of Newport; but since that, not myself alone, but the truth becomes a sufferer, through the sundry reproachful epithets of Mr. Pryne, his brother Grangena, and some that had a hand in my imprisonment, affirming that what I delivered there was blasphemy." It has been stated by some that Hobson was imprisoned for preaching against infant baptism, and by others, that he was a fifth monarchyman; but as these discourses turn simply on the subject of religious experience, they afford no clue to elucidate the question in dispute; in 1653, Captain Paul Hobson was promoted to the rank of Lieutanant Colonel.

We know not that Sir Samuel Luke preached, there is however an opinion supported by respectable authority, that he is the hero whose feats are described in Butler's Hudibras. This exquisite satire, the Don Quixote of English literature, was designed to ridicule the two factions of the opposition; and as Butler was well known to Luke, (it is said he had resided with his family) there is nothing save the sin of ingratitude, to render it improbable for Sir Samuel to have been the butt of the poet's ridicule. There are scattered throughout the poem, references to several incidents in Luke's life, as well as the peculiarities of his person, and one couplet is supposed to mark his name unequivocally.

Luke the supposed Hero in Hudibras.

> 'Tis sung there is a valiant Mamaluke,
> In foreign lands ycleped ....
>   [Sir Samuel Luke.]

for so the chasm has been supplied by the writers of the General History.

But perhaps the design of Butler would hardly allow him to confine his satire to the conduct of one individual, when he wished to expose the follies of a party ; or even in doing so, he might occasionally avail himself of a pointed reference to a man of such eminence as Sir Samuel Luke, and this perhaps was all the satirist ever attempted or designed.

Sir S. Luke's Death.

Sir Samuel Luke lived to see the production of the Second Canto, but before the completion of the work, it ceased to be a matter of personal interest to the Knight, whether he was or was not the subject of Butler's caricature, for dying in August, 1670, he was on the 30th of that month, buried in the parish church of Cople ; and on the pavement of this church, his grandson George is commemorated as " The last Luke of Wood End:"*

We repeatedly meet with complaints of the conduct of the parliamentary forces garrisoned in this county. The Rev. Samuel Maccarnesse,

---

* There is a vague tradition, that while Sir Samuel Luke was governor of the garrison, he fought a duel with the Knight whose helmet, sword and gauntlet, are in the chancel of Stanton Barry Church.

Rector of Stanton, who resided at Great Linford, Rev. Samuel
Maccarnesse. having become obnoxious to the soldiers of the garrison here, they sought his life, and he was compelled to fly from his living, and but narrowly escaped falling into the hands of his enemies. On the restoration, he returned to this country, and some years afterwards, died in great poverty at Stony Stratford. His grandson was a barber of that town, and a great grandson was Rector of Haversham; the barber used frequently to relate the sufferings his Grandfather underwent through his attachment to his sovereign. Walker relates "that the Rector of Tyringham, the Rev. Anthony Tyringham, met with such Rev. Anthony
Tyringham. barbarous usage from the parliament soldiers as almost exceeds belief. He was seized with his two nephews by a party of Dragoons from Ailsburry, near Stony Stratford, who took away their horses, and plundering them of their clothes and money sent them prisoners to their garrison. In the way their guards rifled them again, and because they did not strip themselves fast enough, one of them cut Mr. Tyringham on the head through his hat, and another fired a musket at his nephews: which not contenting them, two of them ran to the body and complained of their resistance, their captain named Pollard, ran, and in his passion made at Mr. Tyringham and almost cut his arm off; carrying them on still to Alisburry, his guard plundered them of their boots, jerkins, hats and caps, and at length brought them thither, where the Surgeons next day cut off his arm; whether he survived this hurt or not, we find not, but sure we are he lived not to be restored to his preferment, nor to see his guard hanged, as he told them he hoped to do."*

These and similar outrages caused a representation to be made to parliament, the result of which was, the house granted Martial Law on the second of February, 1646, to the garrison at Newport and Aylesbury, that the army might be kept in a better state of discipline. The honorable Arthur Annesley by this time had become a supporter of the parliament; at the commencement of the wars he was in the King's service; Wood says he took both the covenant and the engagement, but this statement has been doubted by some. Mr. Annesley's talents and fitness for business, led to his being employed in Ireland as a commissioner of the parliament, and in performance of this duty we meet with his name as an attesting witness to several state papers relative to the affairs of that part of the kingdom.

Honorable Arthur Annesley.

Towards the autumn of this year (1646) this neighbourhood had been in some measure

* Mr. Tyringham appears to have survived this injury for some years, as in the register of burials at Tyringham Church, are the following entries: Mrs. Alice Tyringham, wife of Mr. Tyringham, Rector, June 16, 1659.—Anthony Tyringham, Rector of Tyringham, &c., ob. Aug. 19. Sepr. 21, 1659.

restored to its usual quietude, and on the 17th The Garri-
of October, it was ordered by the House of Com- son.
mons " that the armes and powder at Newport A. D. 1646.
Pagnell be employed by the members of both
houses, that are of the committee of both kingdoms, for the service of Ireland ;" and on the
28th of January 1647, " it was ordered that the
ammunition at Newport Pagnell should be sent
to Ireland, and that the garrison should be slight-
ed."

We must now refer to other events of a more Rev. S. Aus-
local character which took place in this town tin.
during the time of the civil wars. The vicar of
the parish, the Rev. Thomas Webb, dying in the
year 1640, was succeeded by the Rev. Samuel
Austin : who it is supposed by Browne Willis, was
removed from the living by Sir Samuel Luke in
the year 1646, when the Rev. John Gibbs was Rev. J. Gibbs.
put in his place. Mr. Gibbs does not at this
time appear to have been inducted into the living,
as in a lease granted under the common seal of
the hospital, on the 23rd December, 1646, only
the four governors are named ; and from another
lease dated the second of September, 1650, and
containing also only the names of the governors,
it would seem that even at this period, Mr. Gibbs
was not considered to have been the legally
constituted vicar, or his name would have appeared as the master of the hospital; that office,·

being at all times held by the vicar, for the time
being.

The first notice we have of the Rev. John
Gibbs, is in the year 1647, when we find him

Richard
Carpenter.
engaged in a controversy with Richard Carpenter, a native of Newport, on the subject of baptism;
this theme had before excited some attention in
the town, as in 1645, Captain Paul Hobson
was taken into custody by the governor of the
garrison, for preaching against infant baptism.

Carpenter's own account of the affair is, "that
he had been called inwardly, and outwardly re-
called, agreeably to the mixture and even composition of his first, and fundamental calling, to
preach in the parish church, before a very numerous auditory, congealed and consisting of the
more solid and sapid part of town and country. At the close of the sermon, he baptised a
child, but in the sober performance of which
mysterious work, the minister unsettled in place,
and (it seems) in person professing anabaptism,
and suddenly rapted with a vertiginous motion,
interrupted him." The consequence of this in-
terruption, was a public disputation, (a very common occurrence at that period,) and both sides
claimed the victory.

Carpenter especially had the modesty to claim
a triumph, and published an account of the disputation to the world.

In the narrative of the Rise and Progress of the

Independent Church at Newport Pagnell, pub- Richard
lished in 1810, we are informed that Carpen- Carpenter
continued,
ter's book "is written in the highest style of
arrogance, distinguished for a quaintness and
pedantry equally discreditable to him, as a man
of education and literature." The title of the
book is of itself a curiosity. "The Anabaptist,
washt, and washt, and shrunk in the Wash-
ing : or a scholasticall discussion of the much
agitated controversie concerning Infant Baptism;
occasioned by a publicke disputation, before a
great assembly of ministers and other persons
of worth, in the church of Newport Pagnell,
between Mr. Gibs, minister there, and the author,
Richard Carpenter, Independent. Wherein also
the author occasionally declares his judgment
concerning the papists, and afterwards concerning episcopacy. London, printed by William
Hunt." This book, which is a thick 12mo.
and without a date, the author of the narrative
supposes must have been published soon after the
dispute took place ; and it is more than probable, that Carpenter would be desirous of quickly
extending the report of his triumph.

In a history of his native town, Richard Carpenter deserves some notice, otherwise we should
at once dismiss him from our attention. The Rev.
James Granger has given the following account
of him, in his Biographical History of England:
Richard Carpenter was about three years a

scholar of King's College, in Cambridge, and studied afterwards in Flanders, Artois, France, Spain and Italy. He was sent into England by the Pope to make proselytes, but from the natural inconstancy of his temper, and the flexibility of his principles, he soon turned protestant, and was presented to the vicarage of Poling, in Sussex. He was alternately a papist and a protestant three times afterwards, and died in the communion of the church of Rome. He is very differently represented in his portraits, in one he appears like a dull and formal clergyman, in another with all the spirit of an enterprising missionary. His writings are a medley, perfectly suitable to his character. He was living in 1670. Some particulars of this author's personal history, are to be found in a curious work, entitled "Experience, History, and Divinity." He tells us in his book, in which he speaks with great freedom, of the corruption of Rome, that his *whole heart* was never converted to that Church, and we are sure that it was never half converted to the Church of England. Before I take my leave of Richard Carpenter, continues Mr. Granger, I shall present the reader with a specimen of his style, it is before the table of errata, at the end of the book just mentioned. " I humbly desire all clean hearted and right spirited people who shall reade this book, (which because the presse was oppressed, seems to have been suppressed, but now at last hath pressed through the presse Richard Carpenter continued. into the publicke) first to restore it by correcting these errata." One would imagine, says Mr. Granger, that Carpenter, during his residence in Spain, had been particularly conversant with books of chivalry. This specimen is exactly of a piece with the following, which was taken by Cervantes, from one of the Spanish romances, and is the style, which is supposed to have turned Don Quixote's brain. "The reason of your unreasonable usage of my reason, does so enfeeble my reason, that I have reason to expostulate with your beauty." Such then being Richard Carpenter, we must not take for more than its worth, his opinion of his opponent, when he calls Mr. Gibbs "a heady enthusiast, a lean lone Pagnell saint, sometimes a member of the University, and somewhat vexatious to the protestant ministers in the circle about him, and says that his friends and allies fixed all their eyes upon him, as the Carry castle, or Behemoth of the country." We have not been able to collect any particulars of Carpenter's parentage, or birth. In a manuscript list of eminent men, natives of Newport Pagnell, he is styled, Richard Carpenter, Jesuit; a term, which in one word seems fairly to delineate his whole life and character.

In the year 1648, the worthy proprietor of the Abbey, Sir Richard Adkins, served the office of Sir R. Adkins. high sheriff for this county; and as in his appoint-

ment he is described as being of Newport Pagnell, it is likely that by this time, the family had
become regularly domiciled at the Abbey.

On the ninth of August, 1648, we find that the
House of Commons gave directions for securing
the town of Newport Pagnell; this was but a
few months before the final issue of the eventful
struggle of that period; nor is it a little remarkable, that inconsiderable as Newport then was,
" its geometrical situation" rendered it of eminent
service to the Parliament, from the time when
Charles planted his standard at Nottingham, to
the moment, when his chequered life was closed
on the scaffold at Whitehall.

In the time of the Commonwealth, marriage
was viewed simply as a civil contract, and
hence it does not appear from the parish register, that Mr. Gibbs ever married any part of
his parishioners, from 1653 when the marriage
register commences, to July 18th, 1657; the
ceremony being conducted by the neighbouring
justices; the magistrates who officiated on these
occasions, being William Hartley, (for whom on
his decease, it is supposed Mr. Gibbs preached
the " Funeral sermon for Mr. Hartley,") Henry
Whitbread, Thomas White of Caldecot, and William Fosket of Crawley, Esquires. Most of these
marriages were published in the parish church
" three preceding Lord's days," one of the marriages is thus entered in the parish register;

" John Knight of Abthorp, in the county of Northampton, and Bridget Neale of Newport Pagnell,
in the county of Bucks., had their contract of
marriage published three market daies, in the
market of Newport, and was married the 20th
day of February, [1654] by Mr. William Hartley,
justice of the peace for the county of Bucks
aforesaid, in the yeare above written."

Though the ashes of the late King were now
mouldering in the tomb at Windsor, and his son
an exile in a foreign land, there were thousands of persons in this country, and several in
this immediate neighbourhood, who were desirous of calling home their exiled Prince, of
restoring him to his throne, and re-establishing of
monarchy in the kingdom of Great Britain.

In the beginning of this year, 1654, a plot was
laid to destroy the Protector, Oliver Cromwell,
at Hampton Court; to seize the Lord Mayor and Mr. J. An-
Aldermen of the city of London, and take pos- drewes.
session of all the forts and harbours in the name
of Charles II., then residing at Brussells. In
this plot Mr. John Andrewes, a younger branch
of the family at Lathbury, was in some measure
implicated. The intention of this party was, to
grant toleration to the catholics, and send heralds
to various parts of the kingdom, to proclaim
King Charles. Upon the discovery of their design, several of the conspirators were arrested
and imprisoned. Andrewes, with the other pri-

Mr. J. An- soners, was examined at Whitehall, but with
drewes. two exceptions, they were all liberated; Gerrard and Vowell, only suffering the penalty of
the law; they were sentenced to be hanged,
but Gerrard being a *gentleman*, petitioned to
be beheaded, which request being granted, he
was beheaded on Tower Hill on the 10th of
July, his less illustrious companion being hanged
on the same day at the Mews Gate. Mr. Andrewes survived this event but a few months,
he died in the spring of the following year, and
was buried in the family vault at Lathbury, on
the second of April. His name alone, is inscribed on a marble slab, near the Stone Stalls,
in the chancel of that Church.

Sir II. An- Sir William Andrewes dying in 1657, was
drewes. succeeded by his eldest son Henry, who as already
stated had been deputy governor of the garrison,
during part of the civil war, and was brother
to the eminent royalist, John Andrewes. Sir
Henry Andrewes married Elizabeth, the widow
of John Drewe, Esq., of Bishop's Canning, near
Devizes: he had six children, five of whom died
in their infancy.

Rev. J. Gibbs In the year 1655, Mr. Gibbs was Vicar of this
parish; as in a lease of some property belonging
to the hospital, under date of 17th October, 1655,
we meet with his name, described as the master
thereof; and that he continued Vicar till the
very eve of the restoration, is evident from a

memorandum written with his own hand in the parish register, dated the 14th of August, 1659, acknowledging the receipt of a sum of money on that day, collected for a fire, and which sum was paid into his hands as the Vicar of the parish.

A.D. 1659.

In the autumn of 1659, the Commonwealth was hastening to its close. Its presiding genius, Oliver Cromwell, had died the year previous, and his son Richard, having for a short period feebly held the reins of the executive government, resigned his authority into the hands of the Rump Parliament, composed as it was of the dregs of the commonwealth party; the constituent members of this assembly were however so disjointed, as plainly to indicate that its days were numbered. Like the last brilliant flicker of the expiring taper the parliament on the rising of the Presbyterian party at Chester, summoned sufficient courage and resolution for the exigence, and was successful in quelling the rebellion, by entirely routing the Presbyterian royalists, and proceeded so far as to offer a reward for the arrest of Sir George Booth, the leader of the defeated party; in this critical state of affairs, Mr. Gibbs shewed himself an active partizan in the support of the rump Parliament.

Sir George Booth being desirous of proceeding to London, determined on making the attempt, and to guard against the risk of falling into his enemy's hands, he disguised himself in a woman's

Sir George Booth.

P

habit, and with two servants, hoped to reach London, riding behind one of them. Newport Pagnell lay in his way, and on his near approach to the town, Sir George sent the single horseman in advance, who went to the George Inn. The servant, as he had been ordered, bespoke a supper for his mistress, who he said was coming after. Ludlow states that " the pretended mistress being arrived, either by the manner of alighting from the horse, or some other action, a suspicion was raised in the landlord's mind that there was some mystery under that lady's dress.' The inquisitive landlord Carter, and his friends, resolved to make a full enquiry into the matter, and for that purpose entered the room where the pretended lady was, but Sir George suspecting their intentions, and being unwilling or unable to resist, made a voluntary surrender. Upon this discovery, Carter and his friends sought the advice of their minister, who was probably well known to many of the leaders of the Parliament, as a man of weight and influence. Mr. Gibbs might have consented, at their request, to convey to the Parliament the report of Sir George Booth's arrest; for we find that he immediately took horse and rode hastily to London; and on his arrival there, proceeded to the House of Commons, then sitting, for the purpose of communicating the intelligence, In the journal of the house on the 29th of August, 1659, we find the following minute of the proceedings. " The house being informed that Mr. John Gibbs, minister at Newport Pagnell was at the door, he was called in, and being at the bar, gave an account to the house of the apprehending of Sir George Booth, the night before, at Newport Pagnell." Sir George was conveyed to London, and committed as a state prisoner to the tower, from which however, owing to the increasing strength of the royalists, he was soon liberated; having regained his liberty, he was zealously employed in bringing about the restoration of the ancient dynasty of the Stuarts to the throne of England; he and his party were greatly assisted in their efforts by the lord of the Manor of Newport Pagnell, (Arthur Annesley) who had by this time Lord Mount-norris. through the death of his father, succeeded to the Irish title of Lord Mountnorris. This nobleman, who, it must be confessed, had been somewhat changeable in his politics, was not entrusted with the confidence of the leaders of the rump Parliament; and probably being disgusted with the dominant faction, and doubtless seeing no probability of a settled state of the country, while under its then rulers, he abandoned his former course of politics, and united with the royalists, to bring about the restoration of the exiled Charles. His Lordship's talents caused him to be chosen president of the council of state, which was constituted for the purpose of conducting the

Earl of
Anglesea
Baron of
Newport
Pagnell.

arrangements for the restoration the Prince, with whom he carried on a correspondence. Soon after the restoration, he was, in addition to his Irish honors, created Earl of Anglesea, and Baron Newport Pagnell, thus becoming a British Peer. In the preamble of the patent, notice is taken of the signal services rendered by him in the King's restoration; he had a considerable share in the King's favor, and was heard with great attention both at council, and in the house of Lords. Ludlow states in his interesting memoirs, that though he had been on terms of most familiar acquaintance with Arthur Annesley, yet when he became a British Peer and placeman, his " condition altered his manners," and it was in vain that he sought his succour and support, on the rising of that storm which drove him from his country, to end his days in the Canton of Berne.

Mr. Gibbs
ejected
from the
Vicarage
A. D. 1660.

While the restoration of Charles was being determined on, circumstances were passing in this town of great local interest; it was about this period, that Mr. Gibbs was ejected from the parish church, from which time, may be dated the existence of a separate Independent congregation in Newport Pagnell. Calamy, in his Nonconformist Memorials, states that Mr. Gibbs was ejected from the vicarage, for refusing to admit the whole parish to the Lord's table; and it is supposed, that this exclusive regulation was highly resented by a parishioner who possessed considerable influence, but being a notorious drunkard, was denied a participation in that solemn ordinance, and that this led to Mr. Gibbs' ejectment from the living. Whatever was the occasion, it certainly took place too long before the act of uniformity, to have any connection with that enactment, which became law on the 24th of August, 1662 ; Mr. Gibbs must have been ejected very early in the year 1660, as his successor, the Rev. Robert Marshall, was in- *Rev. Robert* ducted into the living on the 24th of March, *Marshall.* of that year.

About twenty years ago, a correspondent of the *Rev. John* Gentleman's Magazine, who at that time resided *Gibbs.* in an adjoining parish, offered the conjecture, that Mr. Gibbs' interference in the arrest of the presbyterian leader, Sir George Booth, if not the real occasion, might have had great influence in causing his ejectment from the parish church ; but little weight however can be attached to this opinion, for we have the united testimony of Richard Baxter, and Edward Calamy, that for conscience sake, and for conscience sake alone was Mr. Gibbs ejected from the vicarage.

Mr. Gibbs was possessed of an estate, consisting of two houses, situated on the spot, where the house belonging to the Rev. Thomas Palmer Bull, now stands. One of the houses fronted the street, and the other behind it which looked into the yard, was occupied by Mr.

Gibbs. Adjoining to his premises was a large barn, which tradition informs us, had previously been occupied as a Quaker's meeting, and on Mr. Gibbs being ejected from the church, he retired, with a large portion of his congregation, to this barn, where he was wont to conduct divine service, and which from its retired situation, afforded the worshippers some shelter from persecution; and many a time, doubtless, have the congregation hastily dispersed and escaped through a door which opened into a bye-lane or court, connecting Marsh End with the High Street, and passed through what is now Mr. Bull's garden.

Doctor Waller.

Amongst the victims of this intolerant persecution, was Doctor Waller, a medical gentleman of eminence in his profession, who resided at the house, now the residence of Mrs. Ward. For ten months, to avoid being committed to prison, for the crime of hearing Mr. Gibbs preach, did this gentleman conceal himself in some of the out-offices belonging to his house; and it is said that during this time, when there was public worship at Mr. Gibbs' meeting, he used to leave his retreat, and crossing a fence by means of a ladder, reached unobserved, the back door of the meeting. There can be no reasonable doubt that this persecution extended to others in the town as well as this gentleman; for why should the nonconformists of Newport Pagnell be exempted from persecution more than those who resided in Persecution of Noncon-formists. other parts of the county, many of whom were proceeded against with remarkable severity, and committed to prison. Such was the rigour of the persecution, that after having filled the common gaol, the magistrates were compelled to hire two large houses at Aylesbury, for the purpose of prisons. After three month's imprisonment, they were tried upon a statute of Queen Elizabeth, which made it felony, if after an imprisonment of that length, they did not conform; several were in consequence condemned, but, through the interference of Mr. Kyffin, an eminent dissenting divine, who represented the case to the Lord Chancellor Clarendon, they were all reprieved, and eventually received the King's pardon.

Of Mr. Gibbs' life, either public or private, Rev. J. Gibbs. but few memorials have come down to us ; that he suffered persecution, appears from the following quotation from the "Elegy, on the death of that famous minister of the gospel Mr. John Gibbs, pastor of the Church of Christ in and about Newport Pagnell":

> In persecution, he hath often stood,
> To seal the truths of Jesus with his blood :
> In dangers great, and perils night and day,
> Was he engaged, amongst the beasts of prey ;
> By wicked ones, he often was misused,
> His hair pulled off, his person much abused ;
> The bloody sword against him they did draw,
> Thereby intending his life to destroy ;

But great Jehovah, with his mighty hand,
Their violence and malice did withstand;
And did defend him from his throne on high,
And kept him as the apple of his eye;
To prison and confinement he did go,
With cheerful heart, and countenance also;
With courage great, he valiantly did stand,
To witness for his Lord with heart and hand.

Such is the quaint recital of the sufferings which Mr. Gibbs endured, but whether he was one of the number who were condemned can only be known by searching the state paper office; and such were the perilous circumstances under which the independent church at Newport Pagnell was established.

Dr. Samuel Annesley.

Amongst the two thousand divines who were ejected from their pulpits by the act of uniformity, on the 24th of August, 1662, was Dr. Samuel Annesley, Vicar of Saint Giles', Cripplegate, a near relative of Arthur Annesley, the Earl of Anglesea. Doctor Annesley died in the year 1696, at an advanced age; it may be interesting to state, that John and Charles Wesley, the founders of methodism, were the Doctor's grandsons.

The Plague A.D.1666.

In the year 1666, the Nation was taught a great moral lesson by the Plague, and which in its course, visited Newport Pagnell, as well as other parts of the Kingdom.

The register of burials for this parish, affords some idea of the devastation produced by that tremendous disease in Newport Pagnell. During the first five months of the year, there had been only 35 interments, in June the number was 104, in July 257, in August 205, in September and October 83, in November and December the number was reduced to fifteen; the greatest number of deaths occurred in July, on the 29th of that month nine persons were buried, on the following day 19, and on the next day 12, so that in three days 40 interments took place, and in the whole year there died fourteen times the average number of the preceding, and the two succeeding years; the number of deaths caused by the plague, amounting to 649. In the year 1665, only 37 persons were buried, in 1667, 54, and in 1668, 53; this is a much lower average of deaths than that of the last twenty years, and leads to the conclusion that Newport Pagnell contained at that period a less number of inhabitants than at present; the present average being about ninety. From the number of interments which took place during the plague, it can hardly be supposed that they were all buried in the church yard, * there is a tradition that many of the dead if not all of them were interred in Bury Field.

* It would appear that during the existence of the plague some persons removed from Newport Pagnell. On the floor of the Ladye Chapel in the Church of Great Linford, is a stone bearing the following inscription:

Rev. Thos. Aspin.

During the time of the plague, the Rev. Thomas Aspin, was the Vicar of the parish, he succeeded the Rev. Robert Marshall on the 6th of October 1663.

Viscount Valentia.

By lease, dated 25th June, 1672, the 22nd Charles II. the Right Honorable Arthur Annesley, by his title of Lord Mountnorris, Viscount Valentia, and Baron of Newport Pagnell, in the County of Bucks., as Lord of the Manor, demised to Matthew Annesley, of this town Tanner, all that Fulling Mill Holme, with the appurtenances thereof, which had continued in his possession since 1642; and two years afterwards, we find that he demised some other property, to Thomas White, of Caldecot, Gentleman, who resided at the Mansion House, of that hamlet, or lordship, and of which house there are to this day some slight traces.

Mark Slingsby.

In the year 1674, our townsman Mark Slingsby gentleman, died; he had been one of the governors of Queen Anne's Hospital, and as during the recent repairs at the Church, his name

ΤΕΟΡΑ ΑΝΘΩΠΟΣ *

"Here lye the bodys of Richard and Martha Peter, who bothe were here joyned in marriage Anno 1636, so it pleased God to lay them together in this bed of movld, Anno 1666, both dyinge in this parish, she on the 14th, he on the 16th of Sep., being removed from Newport by reason of a raging plagve. *Matthew* 19. 6.'

* See what is man.

was found burnt into one of the old beams, it is probable that he had been a churchwarden; he left some singular directions concerning his funeral, and was agreeably to those directions, buried in a brick vault, erected in one of his closes in Tickford field. He bequeathed to the poor of this parish two shillings per week, for ever, to be laid out in bread; the only memorial to this gentleman is a wooden tablet in the west porch of the parish church, which bears the following inscription:

MARK SLINGSBY GENT., of this Parish,
Deceased,
Gave two shillings per week for ever, to be laid out in
Bread for the poor of this parish.

"Come happy ones, blest of my Father, come,
Possess the kingdom, your prepared home;
When I was hungry, and you did me feed,
You visited my servants in their need:
What's done to mine, I take as done to me,
And endless glory, your reward shall be.
Anno Domino 1719.

It is probable this tablet was erected by the parish, as a memorial of the bequest, and not by any of Mr. Slingsby's descendents.

Another donor of charitable bequests to the poor of this town, was Miss Margaret, daughter *Miss Andrewes.* of Sir Henry Andrewes, of Lathbury. She was a young lady eminent for her benevolence, and her early piety. Walking one evening in her father's garden, with her cousin Henry, who afterwards came to the estate, she caught a most severe cold, which at length terminated in her death. A short time before she expired, she enquired whether she had any property she could bequeath, and being told that she had, she requested her sorrowing parents, to bestow forty pounds upon the poor of Newport Pagnell, fifteen pounds upon those in her own parish, and that the chancel of Lathbury church might be paved with marble.

A traditionary story is still preserved, that at the time of her death, Charles, afterwards duke of Somerset, was on the road towards Lathbury, to pay his addresses to her, nor does her tender age render the circumstance improbable, as her cousin Miss Browne, was married to Thomas Lord Leigh, of Stonly, in Warwickshire, when she was but two years older.

A biographical memoir of this amiable young lady, was drawn up by Isaiah Davies, the vicar of Lathbury, for the use of her parents, Sir Henry and the lady Elizabeth; who afterwards gave him their "leave to publish it for the good of others"; of this tract, which is uncommonly scarce, the Reverend James Mansell ascertained the actual existence of three copies only, one of which being in the British Museum.

Browne Willis does not make any mention of it, and probably never saw it, for he states that Sir Henry Andrewes married Margaret daughter of Robert Drewe, whereas in the title page, she is termed the Lady Elizabeth ; some account of this young lady was published in 1777, by Dr. Gibbons, in his memoirs of pious women, a work which has been twice republished, with additional lives, by Jerment and Burder.

The whole of the Doctor's information is derived from the above mentioned tract, but he is incorrect in stating that *Mrs.* Margaret Andrewes as he calls her, was an only child, an error which he must have discovered had he carefully read the preface, which, in addressing the Baronet and his Lady, says, "it is doubtless a great honor to nurse up children as you have done this, and many others, to the kingdom of heaven."

The expression only child, an error which the latin epitaph might be the means of orginating, is true in a qualified sense ; for though as we have already stated, the Baronet had six children, five of them died in their infancy, Margaret alone surviving to the years of maturity.

The latin epitaph at the close of the pamphlet was not, perhaps, ever designed to be inscribed on a monument, Dr. Gibbons has annexed the following free translation :

An epitaph on MARGARET ANDREWES,
The only child
Of Sir Henry Andrewes, Bart.,
And the Lady Elizabeth, his wife.

Stop traveller!

And learn in a few words, the true character of that young lady whose precious remains are deposited under this marble pavement; which, in her departing moments, she was desirous should be laid as a sepulchral covering, not only of her own ashes, but those of her ancestors. She was an accomplished person, the hope and love of her parents, and the delight and ornament of her family. Her bosom was the temple of modesty, purity, and benevolence; the pomps of the world she disdained, the powers of Satan she vanquished; for God dwelt in her, and she in God. An angelic band, rejoiced to fulfil the divine order, on triumphal wings bore away the precious gem to its native skies; the casket which contained this incomparable jewel, as it was formed of earth, so it was returned thither, and is here deposited till the appointed day, which shall restore it in immortal glory. Wonder not stranger, that the soul of this excellent person made so short a visit to our world, as her prayers and devout breathings were the wings and gales that wafted her deeply sanctified spirit to the realms on high.

Depart traveller, ponder, and be wise.

Sir Henry carried into effect the last request of his dying daughter, by distributing fifty-five pounds amongst the poor of this and Lathbury parish, and having the chancel of that church paved with marble; the names only, of the Andrewes' who lie there interred, are inscribed upon the squares of white marble, with the exception of Margaret, and her cousin Lady Leigh The inscription to the memory of Miss Andrewes is as follows:

Here lyeth the body of MARGARET ANDREWES,
who gave this Marble Pavement,

She was the daughter of Sir Henry Andrewes, Bart.,
and ye Lady Elizabeth, his Wife,
who died
May ye 4, 1680, in the 14th. year of her age.

Heaven was her element and Christ her love,
Her heart and all her treasure was above,
And hardly would her mind to earth descend,
She nobly scorned whatever had an end.

Her soul, a sacred flame which pierced the skies,
And was to God a welcome sacrifice;
Faith was her life, and prayer was her breath,
The end and answer of the both was death.

But then a veil of modesty she wore,
She was a secret treasure to the poor;
She hated sin which made the devil rage,
But God engaged for her, who did for God engage.

Her soul doth rest above, her flesh below,
Her name remains on earth and shall do so;
Her name still lives and breathes a pleasant scent,
And shall outwear this marble monument.

Near the south west corner of the altar, is Barrones Leigh. the following inscription.

"Here, ELIZABETH LADY LEIGH, Barrones, of Stonly,
In her father's grave lyeth."

This is the lady to whom we have just referred as the Miss Browne who, at the age of sixteen was married to Lord Leigh; this marriage proved as might perhaps have been foreseen, a most unfortunate match, and they lived on uneasy terms. King Charles the second, who frequently interested himself in the private affairs of his nobility, endeavoured to reconcile them, and entreated Lady Leigh to forgive the ill usage she had received from her husband. She fixed her "fine black eyes" upon the merry monarch of England, and after returning thanks for the interest His Majesty had taken in her cause, requested to know whether he would engage to secure Lord Leigh's good behaviour; this the King could not promise, and when they had departed from his presence, observed that he never had seen so beautiful a woman at court. Her portrait was painted by Sir Peter Lely, in the habit of a Shepherdess. Lord and Lady Leigh at length agreed to separate, on September the 20th 1676, when her husband engaged to pay into the hands of Mr. William Andrewes, two hundred and fifty pounds for the disbursement of her expenses. The unhappy Baroness of Stonly survived this event scarcely two years, and on the 16th of June 1678, at the age of 27, sank into an untimely grave: she appears to have died much involved in debt, to liquidate which, and towards defraying her funeral expenses, his lordship paid a further sum of two hundred pounds. Her jewels and plate were in the possession of Mr. William Andrewes, he engages September 26th, 1681, to deliver them up to her mother, (who had married Colonel Temple,) for £30. of lawful English money.

In the year 1657, Willen Manor became by Willen Church. A.D. 1680. purchase, the property of Colonel Hammond, who had the custody of King Charles at Carisbrook Castle; and in 1673, it was sold by the Colonel's daughter to the well known Doctor Busby, who in the year 1680, erected at his own expense, the present Parish Church; he gave a Library for the use of the Vicar, and endowed the living with the rectorial tythes, which had originally belonged to the Priory at Tickford; he vested the advowson in Trustees, directing that they should nominate from time to time a student of Christ Church College, Oxford, who had been educated in Westminster School; and appointed twenty-two lectures on the Catechism, to be preached annually in the Church.

On the death of the Rev. Thomas Aspin, the Vicars of Newport. Rev. John Howard, A. M. Vicar of Stanton Barry, was on the 16th February, 1678, inducted into the living of Newport Pagnell; after having held it two months, he resigned it for Marston Trussell, and was succeeded by the Rev. John Cook; who held it until his decease, in 1688, and was buried in the Parish Church.

On the 10th of February, 1684, the accession Accession James II. of James II., was proclaimed in Newport Pagnell, " with great joy and gladness," and on the following day the like ceremony, was performed in the town of Stony Stratford.

Sir William Tyringham died on the 6th of

August, 1685; he was the elder branch of this
ancient and respectable family, who had resided
in the village of Tyringham for more than five
centuries.   Sir William left an only daughter the
wife of Mr. John Backwell, who survived her
father three years; Mr. Oliver Tyringham was
buried on the 11th of May, 1695; after which
period we do not meet with the surname of
Tyringham

The Earl of Anglesea dying, on the 6th of
April, 1686, in the seventy-third year of his
age, was succeeded by his son James Annesley, the second Earl, who married Elizabeth,
daughter of John, Earl of Rutland, Arthur Annesley, found what many had done before him, that
courtly favor was an honor of uncertain duration;
though he had been caressed by Charles on
his accession, his fortunes began to ebb, and
perhaps presuming too much upon his acquaintance with his sovereign, the result of the
important services he had rendered the king, he
resorted to measures which ended in his downfall,
he was deprived of his place as Lord Privy Seal,
though his enemies were forced to confess that
he was hardly and unjustly treated.   On the
accession of James, the fortune of the Earl
again revived, and though he was a *Lay* Lord,
yet having studied the Laws of his country, with
such diligence, as to be esteemed a great lawyer,
it is generally believed that but for his death, he

would have been appointed Lord Chancellor of
England. It is to the lasting honour of his lordship, that he was one of the first of the English
nobility who collected a fine library, which he
did with extreme care and at a great expense;
his learning and writings, entitled him to a place
amongst the "Royal and Noble Authors."

The revolution of 1688, and the accession of
William and Mary, must have improved the con- Revolution
A. D. 1688.
dition of the nonconformists in Newport Pagnell.
Having acquired some confidence in the improved aspect of affairs, they left the Barn in
which they had long worshipped, and erected
a building on the site of the present Chapel;
this building which adjoined the barn, measured
on the outside forty feet square, and had one
gallery in the front, four seats deep. The
author of the narrative already referred to, sup- Independent
poses that the Meeting House was built about Chapel Built,
1689.
1689, the year when the Act of Toleration passed,
and remarks that "those who raised these walls
having fresh in their recollection the persecutions
they had endured for conscience sake, left in the
wall of the back front, exactly behind the pulpit,
an opening for a door, no doubt intended for the
Minister to make his escape, in case of the appearance of informers."

In the Memoirs of Doctor Lewis Atterbury, Rector of Milton Keynes, we learn that in the year
1693, he was drowned in this parish, in his Dr. Atterbury
A. D. 1689.

attempt to ford the river on his return from London, but of this circumstance we have been unable to obtain any further particulars. The Doctor's portrait is preserved as an heir loom in the Library of the Rectory house at Milton; he was buried under the Altar in that Church. Doctor Atterbury was Rector of Broad Rington as well as of Milton; to both of which livings he was presented during the Commonwealth, but on the Restoration he was politic enough in order to confirm his titles, to be again instituted to both of them. If, as generally stated, his son, Lewis Atterbury was born on the 2nd of May, 1656, at the hamlet of Caldecot, the Doctor must have resided in this neighbourhood previous to the 11th of September, 1657, at which time he was inducted into the living at Milton Keynes.

Rev. Thos. Kilpin.
A.D. 1696

The Rev. Thomas Kilpin, A. M. Rector of Great Linford, was buried in the Church, at Newport Pagnell, on the 10th of March, 1696; he was probably a son of "Thomas Kilpin who gave forty shillings per annum, to twenty poor families of this parish payable for ever on the 13th day of February yearly, out of the rent of a Tenement in the High-street," then in the occupation of Thomas Kent, and now the property of Mrs. Rose.

Sir Henry Andrewes dying at the age of 72, was buried in the family vault in Lathbury Church, on the 27th of August of this year. His nephew Sir Henry Andrews, A. D. 1696. Henry, who succeeded to his estates, was a son of Mr. Edward Andrewes, of Buckingham, a younger branch of the family of Lathbury, and it is from this branch, the present proprietor of Great Linford, Henry Andrewes Uthwatt, Esq., is lineally descended.

By the death of Sir Richard Adkins in the Sir Richard Adkins, A. D. 1689. year 1689, the Abbey at Tickford with the other estates in this parish belonging to the family, devolved upon his son, the second Sir Richard Adkins who was a Member of Parliament for this county, and Colonel of a foot regiment; a pair of large drums belonging to him are still preserved. Seven years after the decease of his father, and while in the full vigour of his days, he was removed by death, and was buried within the Altar Rails of the Parish Church. Over his remains there is a marble slab bearing the following epitaph; and it is much to be be regretted that the memorial of so distinguished an individual should be in so obscure a situation.

Here under,
Lyeth the body of Sir Richard Atkins, Bart.,
Son of Richard Atkins of Clapham, in Surrey, Bart.,
And Dame Rebecca his wife, daughter of
Sir Edmund Wright, alias Bunckley, of Swakely,
In Middlesex.
The valuable accomplishments of his mind and body recommended him to the love and esteem of all who knew

him, and qualified him for the service of his King and country, in a double capacity, as representative of the gentry of Buckinghamshire, in the High Court of Parliament, and as Colonel of a regiment of foot, under his most sacred Majesty, King William, both which employments he honorably discharged with unbiassed integrity, and unalterable fidelity. He might have been said to be truly happy, being universally beloved by his worthy acquaintance, and blessed with a numerous and hopeful progeny; had not the latter part of his life been clouded with some domestic troubles, caused by the fault of others, not his own, and which ought to be covered with a veil of silence. But these misfortunes, though in a great measure they hastened his end, yet they could not take from him the well deserved character of a true, honest, English gentleman, a man of strict honor, and a hearty lover of his king and country. To preserve the memory of which singular good abilities, and as an instance of her tender affection to him, the Lady Rebecca Atkins, his mother, and sole executrix, has caused this stone to be laid over him. He died November 28th, 1696, in the 42nd year of his age.

Lady Adkins' Gift. A tablet in the west porch states, that about this time, the Lady Rebecca Adkins gave two silver flagons, and one silver salver, for the use of the Communion, and also gave fifty pounds for the putting out apprentice, ten poor children of this parish.

Rev. John Gibbs, A.D. 1699. In the last year but one of the seventeenth century, death put an end to the labours of the Reverend John Gibbs. The loss of their minister seems to have filled the hearts of his followers with grief and dismay, of which the

Elegy* published on the occasion affords ample testimony; Mr. Gibbs was buried near the south door of the Chancel; at the time of his decease, the Rev. Doctor Banks was Vicar. Mr. Gibbs's piety, talents and learning, had secured to him the regard and esteem of a large circle of acquaintance, besides the members of his own congregation; and we learn from the Church Book of the Old Meeting at Bedford, that he was held in high repute by the members of John Bunyan's congregation.

The narrative already referred to gives the following striking proof of the high estimation in which Mr. Gibbs was held; "in the Old Deeds of the now Baptist Meeting House, at Olney, it is expressly mentioned, that no person shall ever be chosen Pastor, who shall differ in his religious sentiments from the Rev. John Gibbs, of Newport Pagnell," Mr. Gibbs appears to have held, somewhat singular notions on the subject of Baptism; in the Church Book at Bedford, he

---

*The Author of the Elegy is unknown. It was printed on a broad sheet for Mark Conyers, Bookseller, Newport Pagnell, and was re-printed about thirty years ago. At the foot of it is advertised Mr. Gibbs's Last Legacy to his Parishioners, price four-pence, and a Funeral Sermon for Mr. Hartley, price sixpence. The Elegy is remarkable for its quaintness and familiarity of expression, so common in the writings of that period; we have only met with one of the original copies.

is called a Catabaptist; and there are some
peculiar distinctions in his manner of registering
the burials in this parish which seems to confirm
the statement. An Altar Tomb was erected
to his memory; of which the top and one end
stone now only remain; it was with great
difficulty that many years ago a gentleman was
enabled to trace the latin inscription, the following is nearly the substance of it:

" This tomb is erected, equally from gratitude and affection,
        Over the spot where are laid the sacred ashes of
                The Reverend JOHN GIBBS;
    A man of a well cultivated mind, wonderful memory,
            Acute judgment, and great learning,
        As well as eminent piety and great integrity ;
        A fervent preacher both to saints and sinners."
[Having been] Pastor of [an Independent] Church, .. years,
        He willingly dismissed his spirit,
                In the year of Christ, 1699,
                And of his age 72."

On one end stone,
            " Here lieth the body of MARTHA,
                The wife of Mr. JOHN GIBBS,
        Who departed this life the 2nd of January, 1704,
                In the 73rd year of her age."

On the other end stone,
    Friendship and gratitude have raised this tomb,
    Wherein his sacred body finds a room :
    Happy his wit, his memory was vast,
    Piously learn'd, and accute to the last.
    Holy as were the purest saints of old,
    In the defence of the true faith most bold ;
    To saints and sinners equally he preach'd,
    And God's own church as faithfully he teach'd.

Within the last few years a handsome Monument has been erected in the Independent Chapel, to the memory of Mr. Gibbs. There is extant a sermon of Mr. Gibbs's preached on the occasion of the death of Mr. Maxwell, whose parents were related to Mr. Gibbs, and who were buried in his tomb.

The house in which the Vicar of the Parish The Vicar-
resides, was erected during this year, chiefly at $\overset{\text{age.}}{\text{A. D. 1700}}$
the expense of the Hospital Funds, the remaining part being obtained by voluntary subscriptions; the house is built on the Hospital property, and is the official residence of the Vicar, in his capacity as Master of the Hospital.

In the year 1683, Alderman Sir William Prit- Sir Wm.
chard, President of Saint Bartholomew's Hos- Pritchard.
pital, purchased of Mr. Thomas Napier, the Manor of Great Linford; Sir William died in 1704, and was buried in the Parish Church of that village on the 1st of March. Upon the death of his lady, who survived him fifteen years, the Estates according to Sir William's bequest, came to his nephews, Richard Uthwatt and Daniel King, Esquires, the latter having sold his share of the property to Mr. Uthwatt, that gentleman became the sole proprietor.

In this year the office of High Sheriff, for the Mr. Henry
county, was served by Mr. Henry Andrewes, $\overset{\text{Andrews,}}{\text{A. D. 1706.}}$
of Lathbury, the Baronetage had become extinct on the death of the late Sir Henry. Mr. An-

R

drewes is said to have planted with his own hand, the famous horse chestnut tree in Lathbury, under which two troops of horse found shelter during a storm.

Darcy's Charity.

It was in the same year that Mrs. Elizabeth Darcy, (formerly the wife of Mr. Richard Edmonds, Surgeon,) gave to this parish two shillings per week, to be paid out of two closes, called Connygrey closes, lately rented by Alice Wadsworth, at £5. per annum, to be laid out in bread for the poor of Newport Pagnell, for ever; in the year 1759, the rent was advanced to £9. and in 1800, was increased to £16. per annum.

Bury Field. A. D. 1712.

It appears that in the spring of 1712, previous to the opening of Bury Field Common, the attention of the inhabitants of Newport Pagnell, was drawn to the subject of the common rights of that estate, upon which occasion the following handbill was printed for general circulation.

"According to the last Survey taken of the Manner of Newport-Pagnell by the King's Commissioners and principal Inhabitants of the said Manner upon-their oaths It is thus inrolled viz

ALSO the Jury aforesaid present that the Inhabitants of the Town and Manner of Newport aforesaid as well within the Burrows as without always Time out of Mind were used to put their Cattle into a Field there called Bury Field when they would yearly after the 3d Day of May there to stay and pasture until the Feast of St. Thomas the Apostle to pay therefore to the Lord or his Farmer the

Sums of Money undermentioned viz For the Pasture of a Bury Field. Bullock Cow or Heifer 12d for a Breeder 6d for a Mare or Gelding 20d for a Colt under 3 Years old 16d from the 3d Day of May until the Feast of St. Michael the Archangel and to pay for the Pasture of every one of the said Cattle from the Feast of St Michael untill the Feast of St Thomas the Apostle half the aforementioned Rates.

Also the said Jury present that the Farmer of the Lord of the said Field called Bury-Field hath not used nor ought to take or put in any other Cattle in the said Field called Bury-Field there to depasture between the 25th Day of March and the Feast of St Andrew but only those so put in by the Inhabitants of the Town according to the Custom of the said Town.

Also the said Jury present that the Inhabitants of the said Manner always time out of Mind used to buy and have of the Lord's Farmer of the said Manner all the Hay yearly growing cutting and coming off and in the said Meadow of Newport aforesaid called the Bury-Mead and to pay therefore for every Acre 3s (the Meadow Ground there being in the said Meadow belonging to a Farm called Mounts only excepted) and that the Lord's Farmer ought not to put or permit any Cattle to go in the said Meadow called Bury-Mead after the 25th Day of March until the said Meadow be mowed and all the Hay carried off there.

Also the said Jury present that upon then viewing and reading an ancient Book being a Survey of the said Manner taken Anno Dom. 1551 in that Book it was mentioned amongst other Things to be presented upon the Oaths of several ancient Tenants of the said Manner that for the Want of sufficient Grass in the said Field called Bury-Field that the Inhabitants of Newport aforesaid ought to put their Cattle in the Pasture there called the Kickle and that if all the Hay growing and coming off the Meadow called Bury-Mead should not be sufficient to supply their Necessity they were used to have Hay in the Meadow called King's-Holm for 2s 8d per Acre and in the Meadow called the Kickle-Mead for 3s 4d per Acre."

A true Copy taken May 14, 1712.

One of these hand bills is preserved with the records in the parish chest; it does not appear when the inquisition referred to was held, but it was probably at an earlier period than the publication of the hand bill.

Doctor Banks. A. D. 1716

The Vicar of this parish, the Rev. Doctor Thomas Banks, who took his benefice here on the 2nd of March, 1688, finding himself unfit for the due performance of his duties, by reason of his increasing age and infirmities, resigned the living, and on the 7th June 1716, was succeeded by his son, Lowde Banks A. B.; the Doctor survived his resignation but a few months, and dying in the following December, was according to Browne Willis, buried here without any memorial.

Dr. Lewis Atterbury.

It was about this time that Dr. Lewis Atterbury founded and endowed a Girls' School in this town; for many years before his death, he himself paid the School Mistress £10. per annum and provided a house for her to live in. The School House is situated in the Paggs Court; it is an old fashioned brick building, originally designed for a workhouse ; over the doorway is a stone, bear- ing the following inscription ;

" For even when we were with you, this we commanded you, that, if any would not work, neither should he eat." 2 Thess. III. 10.

There are twenty girls on the endowment, who are taught to write, read, and sew plain work. We do not know what induced Doctor Lewis Atterbury to found a School in this parish; the fact seems to corroborate the statement that he was born here. This celebrated divine was educated under Doctor Busby, at Westminster School, from whence he removed to Christ Church, Oxford ; and in a few years after he had taken holy orders, he was advanced by a rapid succession of preferments. He was appointed one of the six preaching Chaplains to the Princess Anne, of Denmark, at Whitehall and Saint James's, which appointment was continued after the Princess had ascended the throne, as well as during the early part of the reign of her successor George I.; it is said he was greatly annoyed, that his brother the Bishop of Rochester, would not make him Dean of that place, and an interesting correspondence took place upon the subject. Doctor Lewis Atterbury, died at Bath, on the 20th of October, 1731; in his will he gave some few books to the Libraries at Bedford* and Newport Pagnell;

*This Library which contains many valuable books, has

he charged his estate for ever, with the payment of Ten Pounds annually, for the support of the Girls' School, he remembered some of his friends and left a respectful legacy to his "dear brother in token of his true esteem and affection," probably as a proof of his entire forgiveness, and made the Bishop's son, Osborne Atterbury, heir to all his fortune, after the death of his grand daughter, who did not long survive him. But Doctor Lewis Atterbury's career, however prosperous, was not so brilliant as that of his brother Francis, who was perhaps one of the most remarkable men who were natives of Newport Pagnell and its vicinity.

Francis Atterbury.

Francis Atterbury was born at Milton Keynes, March 6th, 1663, and like his brother Lewis, was educated under Doctor Busby, and in 1681, was elected to Christ Church, Oxford. He soon became eminently distinguished for his politeness, wit, and learning ; and following his wary father's advice of marrying into a family of interest, " a Bishop's, Archbishop's or Courtier's," he married Miss Osborne, a distant relation of the Duke of Leeds. Oxford offering too confined a sphere for his ambitious designs, after ten years resi-

been lately removed from Saint Paul's Church, and placed in the Bedfordshire General Library. The Library at Newport Pagnell is in the custody of the Rev. George Morley, as the Master of Queen Anne's Hospital.

dence there, he removed to " another scene, and
another sort of conversation," and made his home in London, where his pulpit eloquence quickly brought him into notice; he was successivly appointed Preacher, at the Bridewell Chapel, Lecturer at Saint Bride's, and Chaplain to William and Mary, and eventually became the most popular and celebrated preacher of his day; but some of the doctrines he taught involved him in controversy with several of his contemporaries. Patronized by his sovereign, the Queen of the Augustan age of English literature, Doctor Francis Atterbury, was on the flood tide of fortune; higher honors awaited him, he became Bishop of Rochester, and was in expectation of being translated to an Archbishoprick ; but the death of his Royal mistress in 1714, put an end to his preferment and was indeed the first bitter ingredient of his overflowing cup.

George I. had a personal dislike to the Doctor, nor was this dislike in anywise lessened by the Bishop's mistaken policy in the way he sought to conciliate his Sovereign's aversion. Thus frustrated the divine became merged in the politician, and from this moment he became a violent partizan. At first he covertly sided with the Jacobites, but he soon passed the rubicon, and refused to sign the " declaration of the Bishops"

In 1722, being suspected of being engaged in a plot to bring in the Pretender, the Bishop was

His Trial. arrested and committed to the Tower; but such were his commanding talents, that when examined before the Council, he was treated with civility and respect : the populace, however, treated him with less ceremony, they hooted and pelted him through the Streets of London, as he passed in his carriage from the Tower to take his trial in the Lords. The Bishop was accused of attempting to place a Popish Pretender on the Throne of the Realm of England, the trial was of great length, Atterbury's mind rose with his circumstances, his defence was a masterly display of oratory, and has always been spoken of as one of his most brilliant productions; but notwithstanding this, and the efforts of those in the house who espoused the cause of the Pretender, the Bishop was found guilty, sentenced to perpetual exile, and for ever banished the realm. While in the Tower, he was visited by several of his acquaintance; to Pope, one of his most intimate friends, he presented as a parting memorial an elegantly bound Bible; and on the 18th of June, 1723, Bishop Atterbury quitted our shores. During his exile, no one was allowed to communicate with him, without special leave obtained under the sign manual, and after nine years banishment, he died at Paris, on the 15th of February, 1732; his body was brought over to England, and buried in a very private manner in a Vault, which he in his life time caused to be erected in

Westminster Abbey, when, in the days of his prosperity, he was Dean of that Cathedral.

It has been frequently thought that the proceedings against the Bishop were at any rate arbitrary, if not altogether illegal; but be this as it may, all admit him to have been a man of transcendent learning and talents. Blair speaks of his sermons " as a model of correct and beautiful style, besides having the merit of a warmer and more eloquent strain of writing, than is commonly met with."

Doctor Francis Atterbury left behind him two or three Children; one of them, Osborne Atterbury, was advanced to some dignity in the Irish Church, and was the only descendant of the Bishop who left any surviving issue; he does not appear ever to have interfered in the management of the Girl's School at Newport, although empowered so to do.

The Rev. John Gibbs was succeeded by Mr. Tingey; who in the year 1709, exchanged pulpits with the Rev. John Hunt, of Northampton. Mr. Hunt was a man of considerable talent, author of several works,* and after continuing here fourteen years, removed to Tunstead, in Nor-

---

* Infants' right to Baptism, 1704. The Saint's Treasury, a discourse on the glory and excellency of the person of Christ, 1704. Vindiciæ veræ pietatis; or, evangelical sanctification stated, 1719. The doctrine of God's decrees stated, and his righteousness vindicated, 1726.

folk, and was succeeded by his son, John Hunt, at whose ordination, Doctor Calamy took part in the service. In 1735, Mr. Hunt left Newport Pagnell, and became pastor of the Church at Hackney, of which the Reverend Matthew Henry had formerly been Minister.

Doctor Doddridge. About the time of Mr. Hunt's removal from Newport Pagnell, a circumstance occurred which had nearly proved fatal to the independent interest in this Town; the chapel had been erected on an estate, belonging to a principal member of the congregation, but the ground on which it stood had never been properly conveyed to Trustees, and the owner of the estate becoming a bankrupt, the Chapel was seized upon by the creditors. In this emergency Doctor Doddridge, an intimate friend of Mr. Hunt, generously came forward, purchased the Chapel of the creditors, and conveyed it to proper Trustees, and by his activity and influence, the necessary funds were soon raised. In the Gentleman's Magazine, March, 1790, there appears a Letter addressed by Doctor Doddridge to the Rev. Mr. Needham, of Hitchin, asking that gentleman's "advice and assistance to the poor people at Newport Pagnell."

Browne Willis, in his manuscript notes of this Parish dated 1735, states that at that time the number of families residing at Newport Pagnell, amounted to between five and six hundred, and the number of souls to about three thousand; in Population A. D. 1735. another statement he gives a somewhat larger population, making the families amount to between six and seven hundred, and the number of souls between three and four thousand. In the census taken in 1841, the result was as follows: Houses 738, Males 1704, Females 1864, Total 3568.

But to return to the family of the Annesleys. The Annes-ley James, the second Earl of Anglesea, does not appear to have made so considerable a figure in the political world, as his father Arthur Annesley, whom he survived but four years, and was succeeded by his son James, whose only daughter married Sir Constantine Phipps, Baronet, an ancestor of the Marquis of Normanby. James, the third Earl, died in 1710, and leaving no male issue, his estates and honours descended to his brother John. This nobleman was a man of great parts and honour, but dying without issue the same year, he was succeeded by his next Brother, Arthur Annesley, who, on the demise of the Crown, in 1714, was one of the Lord's Justices, to administer the affairs of this kingdom, until the arrival of King, George I., and His Majesty on coming to the throne, appointed him Privy Councillor for both Kingdoms. In 1721, he was elected in full senate High Steward of the University of Cambridge, where he had received his education, and which,

he had represented in three parliaments; on his
death in 1737, the honours and estates were
claimed and taken possession of by Richard, the
younger son of Richard Annesley, third Lord
Altham, Dean of Exeter, the late Earl's brother.
Lord Altham's elder son Arthur Annesley, fourth
Lord Altham, who died some years before his
Uncle the late Earl, was a man of the most
abandoned and dissolute habits; he married
Mary, a natural daughter of John Sheffield,
Duke of Buckingham, by whom he had issue,
James, an only son, to whom at the death of the
Earl in 1737, the title of Earl of Anglesea and
Baron Annesley of Newport Pagnell, should have
descended.   Lord Altham treated his Lady with
such cruelty as to drive her from her home; nor
would he allow her to enjoy in her retirement the
society of her child, scarcely even permitting
her to see him, though not having as yet abandoned all paternal affection, his Lordship had
his son educated in a manner becoming his
station.

Lord Altham's career of vice was indeed a
downward course; after a succession of crimes
he abandoned his child, and the life of this truly
" Unfortunate Young Nobleman," is one of the
most romantic stories in the domestic annals
of Great Britain.   Lord Altham having wasted
his substance in riotous living, it is no wonder
he began to be in want; his extreme neces-

Marginal notes:

Richard Earl of Anglesea.

James Annesley.

Lord Altham.

sities led him to attempt to raise money by the sale of his reversionary interest in the family estates, but his abandoned character, coupled with the non-age of his son, rendered this difficult, if not altogether impossible. In an evil hour it was suggested to Lord Altham, and agreed to by his brother Richard, (the heir presumptive to the estates,) that the child should be removed to some distant and obscure place of confinement, and then soon after to raise a report of his death; he was accordingly sent away, and in a short time it was reported that he was dead.

Just as Lord Altham's difficulties were about to be removed, an obstacle presented itself in the person of his child, for the youth had a determined spirit, and escaping from his confinement, made his way, though secretly, to Dublin, where his father resided; but he was deterred from going home from a fear that a woman at that time living with his father, would betray him into the hands of those who were bent upon his destruction.

Young Annesley continued undiscovered in Dublin for two years, during which time his means of procuring subsistence was very precarious, but not perhaps less so than that of his father, who in the month of November, 1727, died suddenly and so miserably poor, that though an Irish Peer, and heir to an English Earldom, he was buried at the public expense.

James Annesley.

Richard Annesley, the younger brother of the fourth Lord Altham, and heir presumptive to the estates, had proceeded too far in his villany to be now checked in his career, and taking advantage of the non-age and helpless condition of his nephew, the rightful heir, seized upon all the papers of his deceased brother, and assumed the title of Baron Altham. In doing so he had to contend with obstacles to which, however, his craft and money were adequate; there were many to whom the facts of the case were notorious; Garter King at Arms, went so far as positively to refuse to enrol the certificate of the late Lord having died without issue; but, notwithstanding, " through means well known and obvious," Annesley's efforts were crowned with success, and his claim to the Irish Peerage admitted. Lord Altham, however, felt that he held his honours and estates by a feeble tenure while his nephew, James Annesley, continued in this Country, he resolved therefore to have him kidnapped, and sent as a slave to the Colony of America. To accomplish this design, he employed several ruffians as spies to search out the retreat of this unhappy youth; who for some time successfully eluded their vigilance; but being at length discovered, an attempt was made to seize him, in which his uncle personally assisted, but the affair taking place near one of the great markets in Dublin, an honest butcher, named Purcell, with the assistance of some of his neighbours, rescued him by main force from the hands of these mercenary villains. Young Annesley's respite was but of short duration ; his uncle had too much at stake to be thus frustrated in his designs ; his agents once more discovered the hiding place of the youth, they succeeded in capturing their victim, and dragging him on board a ship bound for Newcastle, on the Delaware River, he was conveyed to America, and sold as a slave to one Drummond, a rich planter. "Truth is stranger than fiction," or who could give credit to the statement that the descendant of an illustrious line of Nobles, himself an Irish Peer and presumptive heir to the Earldom of Anglesea, and the Barony of Newport Pagnell, should become a slave in a Colony of that Empire of which he was born to be a Legislator !

The term of James Annesley's bondage was limited to thirteen years, but his sufferings and privations were greatly increased by his frequent attempts to regain his liberty. At the expiration of the period, being by this time twenty-five years old, he hired himself as a common sailor to a trading vessel bound for Jamaica, and there having entered on board one of His Majesty's Ships under the command of Admiral Vernon, James Annesley openly declared his parentage and pretensions. It was most fortunate for An-

James Annesley, kidnapped.

Sold as a Slave.

nesley, that there were several officers in the fleet who knew him when a boy, and were acquainted with his circumstances; through the Admiral's intervention, he was sent to England, where he arrived either in September or October, in the year **1741**.

Four years prior to this event, Lord Altham had become possessed of the honors and estates of the Earl of Anglesea; so that by the time of Annesley's return to England, his uncle was Lord of the Manor of Newport Pagnell, and owned the property in this town which belonged to the elder branch of the family.

Soon after Mr. Annesley's return to this Country, he published "the memoirs of an unfortunate young nobleman," a book now very scarce and rare. Banks speaks of it as a "work replete with circumstances of the most singular and curious nature" Young Annesley's misfortunes excited the most extraordinary and intense interest; and he met with liberal assistance from several influential and wealthy individuals, who heartily espousing his cause, rendered him their support in his efforts to wrest the usurped possessions from his fearfully formidable rival. It is said, that amongst his supporters was a Mr. Cripps, Jeweller, in Fleet Street, a native of Newport Pagnell, whose eagerness to serve Mr. Annesley, involved him in pecuniary difficulties.

The Earl of Anglesea beginning to suspect

that Mr. Annesley might succeed in establishing James Annesley. his claim to the property, had determined on surrendering the titles of Anglesea and Altham, and retiring to France, if Mr. Annesley would allow him two or three thousand a year, but on the first of May in the following year, a calamity befel young Annesley near the town of Staines, in Middlesex, which was seized upon by his uncle the Earl, in the hope, that by a great outlay of money, he should at once crush all the pretensions of his opponent, and so retain the quiet possession of his property.

A man named Egglestone being killed by the accidental discharge of a gun which Mr. Annesley was carrying, the Earl of Anglesea, by a remarkable train of events, succeeded in having his nephew, "James Annesley, Esq. and Joseph Redding,* tried at the Old Bailey for the murder of Thomas Egglestone." The trial took place on Saturday the 15th of July, 1742, the Earl appeared in person on the bench and endeavoured to intimidate and brow beat the witnesses, and to inveigle the prisoner into destructive confessions; but the jury returned a verdict of "chance

---

* Redding was game-keeper to the Lord of the Manor, Sir John Dolben, of Finedon near Wellingborough; Egglestone and his Son were poaching in Sir John's water, Redding attempted to take away a casting net, Mr. Annesley came to his assistance and in the struggle his gun went off by accident.

T

medley." In the report of the trial which long
excited the attention of the public, it is stated
that "mad with rage at this disappointment
was his uncle, and impatient to vent the
malignity of his soul he ran out of court, a con-
tinual volley of hisses and curses followed him
from every one until he was out of sight."
This trial increased the number of those who
felt interested in the fortunes of this young
nobleman, and with their assistance he was
enabled to bring his suit to a trial.

The cause was tried in the Court of King's
Bench, Dublin, on the 11th of November, 1743,
a full report of which was published in a book
now exceedingly scarce.* Twenty-seven Council were employed, fifty-two witnesses were
examined on the part of the plaintiff, and a
great number on the part of the defendant;
the trial occupied thirteen days. On Friday
November the 25th, the three Judges summed
up the evidence at great length, the Jury then
withdrew, and after two hours deliberation
brought in their verdict for the plaintiff; but

* The trial at bar, between Campbell Craigg, Lessee of
James Annesley, Esq., Plantiff, and the Right Honourable
Richard Earl of Anglesea, Defendant. With a Portrait of
the Honourable James Annesley, Esq. Printed by and
for the proprietor R. Walker, in Fleet Lane, MDCCXLIV.
12mo. p. p. 448.

Lord Anglesea seeing that the cause was going against him, had resolved before the trial was concluded, on applying for a writ of error, which being obtained, the verdict was set aside, and further proceedings were in progress, when in the year 1760, Mr. James Annesley died, leaving an infant son, Arthur Annesley.*

The claims of James Annesley remaining unde- Lord cided, his uncle retained the titles until his death, Anglesea. which occurred one year after the decease of his nephew, and on the decease of the young claimant Arthur Annesley, three years after the death of his father, the son of the Earl of Anglesea had a clear indisputable right to all the honors and estates of the family, so far as James Annesley and his infant son were concerned; but no sooner had James Annesley's son been laid in his father's tomb, than Lord Anglesea

* In July 1840, an interesting paper appeared in the Gentleman's Magazine, suggesting the idea that James Annesley's life was the ground work on which Sir Walter Scott's fancy reared the romance of Guy Mannering, and there are certainly two or three striking coincidences which may seem to justify the opinion; but if such had been the case, it is probable that the Great Wizard of the North, would have referred to other and far more marvellous incidents in the life of Mr. Annesley, than the accidental discharge of a gun and the natural delight an honest peasantry would manifest on the return of the right heir to the property, who had been long supposed dead.

met with an opponent to his Irish honors in the person of John Annesley, Esq. who denied the validity of the late Earl's marriage with Juliana Donavan, the mother of the present Earl: but after an investigation which continued nearly four years, the question was determined in his Lordship's favor, and in 1765, on attaining his majority, he took his seat in the Irish house of Lords, as Viscount Valentia, and immediately petitioned for his writ of summons to the English Parliament, as Earl of Anglesea, and Baron Annesley of Newport Pagnell. This writ, on the 22nd of April, 1770, the Peers of this Kingdom refused, the house coming to an opposite conclusion to that of the house of Lords in Ireland ; for judgment was given against him, but in a thin house, and by a small majority. This decision led to the question of Lord Valentia's right being a second time brought before the Peers of Ireland, but although argued for twenty-one days, in a very full house, with examinations at great length, the Lords confirmed their former judgment. Hence by these opposite decisions both turning on the same evidence, his Lordship was able only to enjoy the Irish honors of his family, while the English honors, Earl of Anglesea, and Baron Annesley, of Newport Pagnell, were considered extinct ; in 1793, his Lordship was advanced in the Irish Peerage, to the Earldom of Mountnorris, and in the year 1807, he sold the

Manor of Newport Pagnell to the late Mr. Manor
Hardy, whose son Doctor Hardy, is the present Sold to Mr.
Lord.

Such then is the history of the Annesley family, The Annes-
and such the causes which led to the loss of their
English honors, and the closing of their connection with the town of Newport Pagnell; a place
in which they had possessed property, since the
dissolution of the religious houses, a period of
two hundred and eighty-two years.

The title, Earl of Anglesea, has been conferred
as a Marquisate on the Lord Paget's family; but
the barony of Newport Pagnell still continues
dormant or extinct.

In turning now to matters somewhat nearer Mr. Henry
home, we find that Mr. Henry Andrewes the Andrewes.
last of that name who resided at Lathbury, died
in the year, 1744, and on the 26th of May, was
buried in the family vault of that Church; leaving
no male issue, his estates passed to his four
daughters as coheirs. Ann, the eldest, married
Thomas Harris, Esq, of the City of Winchester,
who died without issue; the second daughter
Elizabeth, married Richard Uthwatt, Esq., of
Rickmansworth; the third daughter, Jane, married the Rev. William Symes, Vicar of Compton Martin, Somersetshire; and Margaret the
youngest daughter, married Alexander Dalway,
of Carrick Fergus, a Captain in the army who
fell at the battle of Fontenoy, in the year 1745.

Mrs. Symes lived some years at Lathbury separate from her husband, and continued to reside there, after her father's decease.

The North Bridge.

Prior to this period, there was only one bridge over the Ouse on the road leading to Northampton; it was a little eastward of the present bridge, one of the original arches still remains in Miss Beaty's Garden; the road after crossing the bridge passed along the close on the east side of the present bridges. In the time of a flood this road was always dangerous, and there is a tradition that Packman's pit, derives its name from the circumstance of a Packman having lost his life there, in attempting to ford the river at the time of a high flood. This inconvenience was in some measure remedied by a bridge erected by Mr. Symes at his own expense on the border of his estate, which was secured from being a public thoroughfare by two portals, the keys of which were kept at Lathbury Mansion, and in the event of a flood the bridge was opened for the convenience of those travellers who chose to pay five shillings for the accommodation; upon one occasion, Mrs. Symes who was a Jacobite, attempted to make use of her controul over this bridge to serve the interest of Charles Edward, the Pretender, who in 1745, was in

Rebellion A.D. 1745.

Scotland collecting an army, with the design of re-establishing the Stuart family on the Throne. The rumour of this rebellion excited the greatest alarm throughout the Country, in which this neighbourhood participated; and on the report that the enemy was advancing towards Newport, many of the inhabitants removed their plate with other valuable goods, and secreted them in the fields and houses distant from the main road; but their fears were groundless, for before the Pretender had crossed the Tweed, the Duke of Cumberland was on his march to decide the question by an appeal to arms; he left London with a numerous army, whose "March to Finchley," afforded a subject for Hogarth's pencil. On the arrival of the army at Hockliffe, a part of the forces marched by way of Stony Stratford, the inhabitants of which place being compelled to open their houses, and to litter down their Kitchens to afford the soldiers a lodging. The division which came through Woburn, halted here for the night, and was quartered in various parts of the Town; sufficient accommodation not being otherwise afforded, the Duke ordered the Parish Church to be broken open, that it might serve as barracks for his men; the Cannon and Baggage were placed in Bury Field. On the following morning, the usual road being impassable in consequence of the heavy rains which had fallen, it was necessary that the portals of the bridge should be opened, and a messenger was sent across the fields to Lathbury to demand the key; but it could not be

Duke of Cumberland.

Mrs. Symes obtained, as Mrs. Symes had ordered her servant to say that she was not in the Country, and that the key was at her town residence in Great Ormond Street.   As the Lady was suspected of being a Roman Catholic, and known to be a violent Jacobite, the Duke considered the denial an insult to himself, and suspecting the real cause of the refusal, he declared that if any man, woman, or child, would say that the inhabitants of that house were Papists, he would plant his cannon against it and blow it to atoms.   No one giving the required information, after a delay of nearly two hours, orders were given to break open and demolish the Gates, and as the men marched through Lathbury, they cut to pieces and destroyed all the trees and hedges belonging to Mrs. Syms, out of revenge for the delay she had occasioned.   It was afterwards known that Mrs. Syms was at Lathbury when the key was refused, but by sending a false report to the Duke of Cumberland she hoped to delay his army until the Pretender might reach Newport, not being aware that Charles Edward had then made but slight progress in his march.

Cannon Corner.   It is generally supposed that one of the Duke's Cannons being injured and there being no person in Newport competent to repair it, it was left behind and placed at the corner of Saint John Street, which has thus acquired the name of "Cannon corner"; but this tradition is some-

what doubtful, as will appear from the will of
Mrs. Tabitha Leverett, widow, and Ironmonger,
of Newport Pagnell, dated the 12th May, 1740,
from which the following is an extract: "I also
give my son Aquila Leverett, one shilling in good
and lawful money of England, and no more, but
the iron back that is in the chimney I now live in,
and the iron gunn that stands in the street, to
defend the corner of the house, for standards for
ever."

The portals on Lathbury bridge were again Lathbury Bridge.
put into repair, but it being desirable for the
accommodation of the increasing traffic* on this
road, that the bridge should be thrown open for
the public, the County Magistrates, in the year
1757, purchased the bridge of Mrs. Symes.

The following is a statement of the amount of
money received at the bridge from 1750, to the
time the portals were removed:

		£.	s.	d.
Memorandum, 1751. That	1750.	38	17	9
Carriages which pay by	1751.	56	3	8
the Year, contribute	1752.	34	2	0
£7. 10s. 0d.	1753.	30	5	0
	1754.	16	0	6
	1755.	29	15	9
	1756.	52	18	9
	1757.	27	16	0

* Amongst other travellers who passed through Newport
Pagnell, was William Hutton, the future historian of Birmingham, who in the 1749, walked from Derby to London,

The extensive repairs which this bridge has lately undergone, have removed all traces of the original structure erected by Mr. Symes.

Rev. H. Gainsborough. The last individual to whom we referred as being the Minister at the Independent Meeting House, in this town, was the Rev. J. Hunt, he was succeeded about the year, 1740, by the Rev. Humphrey Gainsborough, brother to the celebrated portrait painter, and the author of the Latin inscription on the Tomb in the Church yard, to the memory of Mr. Sanderson, a monument which has unfortunately been suffered to fall into decay, a portion of the tablet now only remaining. The inscription was to the following effect:

Sacred to the Memory of
JAMES SANDERSON,
Of Newcastle,
Who died suddenly at Newport,
on his way to his native place,
September, 13th 1745,
On the day of the month on which he was born,
Anno Domini 1706.

Life, like a tale that's told, runs smoothly on,
Charms the vain mind awhile and then 'tis done,
So found poor Sanderson.   He left his native home,
Pleased with the thoughts of gain, but gained his tomb;

he states in his autobiography "I stopped at Newport Pagnel, my Landlord told me my shoes were not fit for travelling; however, I had no other, and like my blistered feet I must try to bear them.

From native soil to this fair spot he came,
Here dyed, but dying left a deathless name;
His sudden and extensive sorrows spread,
Spectators wept, the hearts of lovers bled.
But why? the man was good, the soul released,
Fled up the skies to heaven, with God is blest.
Reader, then know thyself, live but as he,
Die where thou wilt, such glory waits for thee.

In the year 1747, Mr Gainsborough removed to Henley-upon-Thames, where he died suddenly on the 23rd of August, 1776, whilst conversing with some Gentlemen about the locks in the Thames which had been constructed under his direction. He was a man of great mechanical genius, and the inventor of a sun dial, now in the British Museum, which will point the time to a second in every part of the globe; several other of his inventions have since been introduced into general use. Such was his genius, piety, and universal philanthropy, that wherever he was known, he was greatly respected; considerable preferment was offered him in the Established Church, which he declined.*

Mr. Gainsborough was succeeded by Mr. Afflick, and Mr. Fordyce, neither of whom re-

* Mr. Gainsborough possessed as strong a genius for Mechanics as his brother the artist had for painting.—Few men were ever more respected than this worthy divine, he was as eminent for humanity, simplicity and integrity as he was for genius.—*Gent. Mag.* 1788, *p.* 756.

sided here long, nor do we know in what order
they succeeded Mr. Gainsborough; these gentlemen were both Scotchmen, and it was probably
this circumstance, which induced the Scotch
Packmen, who came to this Town to attend at
the Chapel; the lodging house of these men was
the Chequers, and when they attended Chapel
they were in the habit of sitting in the front pew
of the middle gallery. This gallery having at
that time only a railed front, these Scotchmen
had it panelled at their own expense, and for
many years afterwards the pew went by the
name of the Scotchmen's pew.

Mr. Fordyce who obtained celebrity as an
elegant and learned writer, was born at Aberdeen
in 1711: after receiving the early part of his
education at the Grammar School, he was at the
age of thirteen, entered in the Greek Class at
Marischal College Aberdeen; and when but 17
years of age was admitted to the degree of
M. A.; in 1742 he became Professor of Moral
Philosophy in the same College. He was originally designed for the ministry, to prepare himself
for which, the entire purpose of his studies
was directed, and how well he qualified himself for this duty appears in his Theodorus,*

---

* In speaking of his Theodorus a contemporary writer
observed "that the piety of the writer appears to have been
manly, and rational; his sentiments of the divine perfections
exalted and amiable; his knowledge of human nature, and

a Dialogue concerning the Art of Preaching.
He also wrote amongst other works, Dialogues
on Education, and the Treatise on Moral Philosophy published in the Preceptor.

From Aberdeen Mr. Fordyce came to Newport, which he left about 1750, when he made a
tour on the continent, but on his return he was
shipwrecked, and lost his life in a storm on the
coast of Holland; thus ended the career of a
man who had excited the highest expectations
of the future benefits to be derived from his
talents and learning; he had reached only his
forty-first year. He was the elder brother of
Doctor James Fordyce, whose celebrated Sermons to Young People have been translated into
several European Languages.

It will be in the recollection of our readers Mr. R.
that Mr. Andrewes' second daughter married Uthwatt.
Mr. Richard Uthwatt, of Rickmansworth, he
died in the year 1749; he was a Magistrate
for this County, and made extensive collections
for a complete body of heraldry, together with
some documents relating to judicial matters,
consisting chiefly of extracts from, and references to, the Mirror for Magistrates, and
Abridgment of the Common Law: he had also
prepared a plan with materials, for a work on

of the various ways of touching the human heart very
extensive; and his eloquence natural and affecting." *Rees'*
Cyclop., Vol. XV.

Horticulture.　His widow went to reside in London, she became a Roman Catholic, and on her decease was buried in the family vault at Lathbury, on the 2nd of April, 1764.

Mr. Henry
Uthwatt.
A. D. 1757.

Mr. Uthwatt was succeeded by his son Henry, who married Frances, daughter of Sir John Chester, Baronet, of Chichely, by his Lady, the daughter of Lord Bagot. Mr. Uthwatt served the office of High Sheriff of this County in 1755, in which year, by the death of his kinsman, Mr. Uthwatt, of Great Linford, he became possessed of that estate, and went to reside there, he survived this accession to his fortune but little more than two years, and dying in December, 1757, was, on the 31st of that month, buried in the vault of his maternal ancestors. In the North Aisle of Lathbury Church, there is a monument to his memory.

Mr. Uth-
watt, Great
Linford.

Mr Uthwatt of Great Linford, to whose property Mr. Henry Uthwatt succeeded, was a man of great learning and accomplishments, and during his father's life time, had travelled over France and Italy. In the year 1726, he served the office of Sheriff. He was one of the contributors to Fenny Stratford Chapel, where his arms are inscribed on the ceiling: he appears to have assisted Browne Willis, (whose intimate friend he was,) in his collections, and who dedicated his account of Great Linford to Mr. Uthwatt. This Gentleman also made extensive

collections for a complete body of the Peerage,
similar to the work afterwards published by
Edmondson and Banks, which he transcribed
into a folio volume, making draughts of all the
Armorial Bearings, dividing the work into two
classes, the first consisting of the Nobility and private families, and the second of Baronets. He did
not however, live to complete his work, for being
at times disordered in his mind, in a fit of in-
sanity, he made an attempt on his life, and died
in a few hours after on the 8th of August, 1754,
leaving an only daughter, Catherine, the Lady
of Matthew Knapp, Esq. of Little Linford.

By the death of Sir Charles Bagot Chester, in Sir Chas.
the year 1755, the baronetage of Chester became Bagot Chester.
extinct; and dying without issue his estates
descended to his cousin Charles Bagot, brother
to Lord Bagot, who in 1753 had taken the name
of Chester, the estates at Chichely still continue
in this family, the present proprietor being a
grandson of Mr. Charles Chester.

The Rev. Lowde Banks, Vicar of this Parish, Revds. L.
who died in the year 1757, was succeeded by the Banks, and R. Watson.
Rev. Robert Watson ; and in the following year,
a most liberal bequest was made to this parish,
by Mr. John Revis, a native of this town, but Mr. Revis'
who resided in Westminster, he gave twenty Charity.
threepenny, and ten sixpenny loaves, to thirty A. D. 1758.
poor inhabitants, who should attend divine service in the Parish Church, from the feast of All

Mr. Revis. Saints to the annunciation of the blessed Virgin Mary, to be paid for ever out of the rent of two houses in High Street, opposite the Swan Inn. Mr. Revis also built in his life time, and at his death endowed seven alms houses, in the Church-yard, for four men, and three women, who receive the weekly sum of six shillings, a chaldron of coals is given yearly to each inmate, as well as a coat to each man and a gown to each woman.

On his decease Mr. Revis was brought to his native Town for interment, and was buried in a Vault under the north porch, a monument bear-ing the following inscription, has been recently removed to the east end of the north Aisle, immediately over the Pew, appropriated to the inmates of the alms houses.

Sacred to the Memory of
Mrs. Eliz. & Ann Revis,
Daughters of Mr. John Revis, Apothecary,
and Sarah, his wife,
Ann after a very long and painfull illness,
which she bore with a true Christian Patience
and Resignation to the Divine will,
exchanged this life for a better, on Wednesday, Jany. 8th
1755, in the 53[d] year of her Age.
Eliz[th] Died on wednesday Feby. 26, 1755,
in the 60th Year of her age.
Eliz[th] Clark, Daughter of Mr. John Clark,
Apothecary, and Sarah his Wife, Died Friday
Octob[r] 26, 1750, Aged 13 years & 17 days,
And all three lye buried in a Vault in this Porch.
This Monument was Erected by Mr. John Revis,

of Charing Cross, in the Parish of St Martin's in the
Fields, Westminster, Linnen Draper,
to Testifie the great love and Affection he bore
his Sisters, and the Sincere regard he had for
the other.

Among whose Remains now lie those of the above
worthy John Revis, the last of his Father's Family, who
after acquiring a good Fortune with Justice & Honour,
and taking care of his Mother's most distant Relations :
did in his Life Time Erect Seven Almshouses in this
Churchyard, for 4 Men & 3 Women, for ever, and att his
death give a generous Endowment to this his native Town,
in Houses, Land, & Money, to the value of 3700£, and
who was suddenly translated into a better world.

In his Will, Mr. Revis directed his Executors
to invest £150. in the joint names of the Governors of the Charity, who were to meet yearly,
on the 13th July, at Newport Pagnell, to hear
divine service, when a sermon was to be
preached by the Vicar, and the Trustees were
to audit the accounts of his charities; they
were to pay £1 1s. to the Vicar for the sermon, and for reading over such parts of his Will
as related to his charities, which he desired might
be done after the sermon; and he earnestly requested the Trustees of the several other charities of the Parish, to collect the several uses
for which any property had been given to the
parish, that the same might also be read over to
the congregation; by which means, the dona-
tions of the several pious Benefactors would be

Mr. Revis. kept in perpetual remembrance, and it would be a means to prevent any ill use to be made of them.   The surplus money of the interest on the £150. was to be divided as follows : 5s. to the Parish Clerk, 2s. 6d. to the Sexton, and the remainder to provide a dinner for the entertain-

Sir Richard ment of the Governors.
Adkins.
About this period Sir Richard Adkins sold Tickford Park to the Uthwatts, of whom it was purchased by Sir William Hart; upon whose death, his daughter sold it to Mr. Jacques.   On the marriage of this gentleman's Widow with Mr.

Tickford Van Hagen, the estate became the property of that
Park. family, in whose possession it still continues. In the same year, the manor of Caldecot was sold to William Backwell, Esquire, Banker, of London ; in 1769 he bequeathed it to William Harwood, who assumed the name of Backwell ; this estate has since passed into various hands.

Bury Field. ' From this time we no more meet with the name of Adkins in connection with Newport Pagnell ; the Kickles farm, Bury field, and Bury meadow, have also passed into other hands.

Tickford In 1758 Mr. Hooton purchased Tickford Ab-
Abbey. bey, and lived there till his death : during his re-
A. D. 1758. sidence Mr. Hooton erected a family vault in the chapel garden, a retired part of his grounds, and the supposed site of the burial ground of the Conventual Church.   The vault contains two chambers, and is entered by an iron gate in the brick

wall which surrounds it; the wall is octagon, embattled, and about 12 feet high. On the western side of the vault is an obelisk, 25 feet high, containing the following inscriptions :—

This obelisk was erected by Thomas Hooton, to preserve the memory of Sarah, his Wife, Daughter of John Walton, of Spratton, in the County of Northampton, who departed this life the 5th day of December, 1768, and was interred near this place the 10th, aged 47 years.

In this vault are deposited the remains of John Walton Hooton, Son of Thomas & Sarah Hooton, who departed this life December 14th, 1794, aged 31 years.

Likewise of Susanna Hooton, Daughter of Thomas & Sarah Hooton, who departed this life December 1, 1799, aged 44 years.

Likewise of Thomas Hooton Ward, only Son of Philip & Sarah Ward, and Grandson of Thomas Hooton, who departed this life January 22, 1800, aged 2 years.

Likewise of Thomas Hooton, Esquire, who departed this life December 13, 1804, aged 83 years.

The mortal remains of Sarah Ward, Daughter of Thomas Hooton, Esquire, and Wife of Philip Hoddle Ward, Esquire, were deposited in this vault November 27th, 1831. The remembrance of true worth will ever speak for her to whom this last tribute of affection is placed.

On the occasion of a funeral, the service for the dead, as prescribed in the Book of Common Prayer, is performed by a Clergyman; from the circumstance of the ground having been the burial place of the black Monks, the spot is still considered sacred. It is a singular fact, that within the limits of this parish there were four private burial places: one at the Abbey—another in

Tickford Field, where Mr. Mark Slingsby was buried—a third in Marsh-end—and the fourth in Green-end.

That in Marsh-end was in the garden of Mr. William Hooton, a portion of which was designed by Mr. Eaglestone as a burial ground for the Baptist Chapel; and, agreeably to this intention, one Mary Church was buried there; but Mr. Holland Eaglestone being opposed to it, the design was abandoned, and the exact place of interment cannot now be traced.

In Green-end is the tomb of Doctor Renny, a Physician who owned the house now occupied by Mrs. Levi, and adjoining which the monument is erected. Mr. Renny originally practised as a Surgeon, but resigned that branch of the Profession to the late Mr. Rogers. The Poet Cowper, in one of his letters addressed to Mr. Unwin, after speaking of Doctor Samuel Johnson, thus refers to Doctor Renny:—"There is one Doctor at least whom I have lately discovered my professed admirer. He too, like Johnson, was with difficulty persuaded to read, having an aversion to all poetry, except the Night Thoughts; which on a certain occasion, when being confined on board a ship and no other employment, he got by heart. He was however prevailed upon, and read me several times over; so that if my volume had sailed with him, instead of Doctor Young's,

I might perhaps have occupied that shelf in his Doctor Renny.
memory which he then allotted to the Doctor :
his name is Renny, and he lives at Newport
Pagnel."

Doctor Renny left directions to be buried in his
garden ; on his death his desire was accordingly
fulfilled, his friend, the Reverend William Bull,
performing the ceremony. The grave is in the
centre of a raised plot of ground, which is surrounded by a Haha fence, and on one side are a
number of poplar trees ; a plain obelisk in the
centre bears the following inscription, written
by himself :—

P. RENNY, M.D.

Natus XIV. Augusti, MDCCXXXIV.

Denatus XIV. Februarii, MDCCCV.

As in the course of our narrative we have had Browne Willis. A. D. 1760.
frequent occasion to refer to Browne Willis, it
may not be improper to state that he died on the
5th of February, in this year, at his house,
Whaddon Hall, and was buried within the altar
rails of the chapel at Fenny Stratford, which
by his means had been erected by subscription.
He was senior fellow of the Society of Antiquaries in London, and was the author of many
useful and valuable works relating to the ecclesiastical history and antiquities of this kingdom.
. On the 22nd of October, in the following year,
Mr. John Perrott, a native of this town, a Linen

Draper and Laceman on Ludgate Hill, was ca-
pitally convicted for having, on his last examination, concealed his property from the Bankrupt
Commissioners, with intent to defraud his Creditors.   He was executed on the 11th day of
November, in Smithfield, on a gallows erected
for that purpose; his body was brought to Newport Pagnell, and was buried in a tomb in the
Church-yard, which is yet standing.

The circumstances of this case were fully reported at the time in a quarto pamphlet, published in two parts,* a book which certainly
makes some extraordinary disclosures.   But
however improvident Perrott may have been,
(and by some he has been called a swindler,)
Green, in his Spirit of the Bankrupt Laws,
boldly states that Perrott was illegally executed;
and he goes on to say that Perrott's conviction
was " a mistake, yet it unfortunately happened
to be such an one as occasioned him to lose his
life, which he had not forfeited to any law of this
country that I know of."   We learn from the
narrative, that the unhappy criminal is reported
to have evinced great penitence; and it would
almost border on inhumanity to doubt his sin-

* An Authentic Narrative of the Proceedings under a
Commission of Bankruptcy against John Perrott, late of
Ludgate Hill, Laceman.   Published under the inspection
of the principal Acting Assignee.   London; R. Griffiths,
in the Strand, MDCCLXI.

cerity : but certain it is, that he could not by John Perrott.
any means be prevailed on to make any fur-
ther retribution to his injured creditors, though
there is the utmost reason to believe it to have
been in his power. The deficiency in his affairs
amounted to at least £17,000. Amongst the
property which the Bankrupt secreted was a
paper parcel, sealed with three seals, supposed
to contain bank notes ; on his first examination
he stated that the parcel contained some papers
relating to some private transactions between
him and one Holt, of Newport Pagnell, but
in a subsequent examination he swore that the
parcel contained nothing but letters from the
fair sex, which he had since destroyed.

The Minister who succeeded Mr. Fordyce, at Revd. Wm. Bull. A. D. 1763.
the Independent Chapel, was the Revd. James
Belsham, of Bedford. He continued to preach
here until 1763, when he resigned his pulpit, and
was followed by the Reverend William Bull, at
that time a Student at the Academy at Daventry,
under the direction of Doctor Ashworth. Mr.
Bull, who had preached his first sermon in this
chapel, was at the completion of his studies, invited by the Church and Congregation, to become
their Pastor. The invitation being accepted, he
was ordained on the 11th of October, 1764.

In the year 1768, Mr. James Leverett, White- Mr. James Leverett.
smith, of this place, gave to the Parish Church
the Branch which hangs nearest the organ loft ;

and in the following year gave an altar piece and rails for the chancel.   A few years afterwards, Mr. Edward Whitton* added to the endowments of Newport Pagnell by a bequest of £100., to be invested by his Executors in the Old South Sea Annuities in the name of four Trustees, the Vicar always to be one ; who, with the interest thereof, were to purchase bread for the poor on the 5th day of January, for ever.

Mr. Whitton.

Mrs. Symes, of Lathbury, during her residence in Great Ormond Street, London, in 1774, was publicly accused of beating and starving her servants, which gained her the name of " Brown-rigg." The Public Advertiser, 17th February, contains the following account of the proceedings held the day previous at the office in Bow Street :—" Ann Smith, a girl of fifteen, brought a charge against Mrs. Symes, a lady of fortune, of Lathbury, in the county of Buckingham, now in London, in the West-end of the town, for cruelly beating her at divers times, and frequently keeping her for many hours together in

Mrs. Symes.

* Mr. Whitton, who resided at Northampton, was a Gentleman of considerable property ; and after having declined trade himself, generously lent sums of money, at a low rate of interest, for the mere purpose of assisting industry.   It was to this gentleman that Perrott was mainly indebted for his introduction into trade—for his support in the course of it—and for the credit he afterwards obtained. How shamefully Perrott abused Mr. Whitton's generosity, appears in the narrative already referred to.

the yard belonging to her house, during the late Mrs. Symes. extreme cold weather, The facts being clearly proved, the girl was released from her apprenticeship, and the overseers were advised by the bench to lodge an indictment against her mistress."

It is somewhat singular, that when the Overseers examined into the affair, they found the truth so different from what had been stated at Bow Street, that they apologised to Mrs. Symes, enquiring whether they had not mistaken the house, and departed, satisfied that the whole was an imposition. Mrs. Symes died in London, and was buried in her family vault at Lathbury on the 26th October, 1778, leaving an only daughter, Jane, who inherited her mother's moiety of the estate at Lathbury.

In the third week of March, in the year 1779, John Howard. John Howard, in one of his tours to "take the A. D. 1779. guage and dimensions of misery," visited Newport Pagnell, where he says he "regretted to find that the only Bridewell for the county of Buckingham consisted of two unwholesome cells, from which the prisoners had recently escaped, as there was every opportunity for them to do, the Governor's house not being near the Prison." The Bridewell stood near Tickford-bridge, and appears to have been considered merely as a cage or temporary lock-up house.

Amongst the celebrated characters who were

connected with Newport Pagnell was Mr. John Henderson.   He was born in Goldsmith Street, Cheapside, in February, 1747; his father dying in the following year, his mother was left with a very slender pittance, and two sons totally dependent upon her.   After her husband's death Mrs. Henderson, whose maiden name was Cripps, came to reside at Newport Pagnell, her native town, and where her relations lived : by a close attention to economy, Mrs. Henderson was enabled to support herself and family upon the interest of less than a thousand pounds.   Here, with no other tutor than his mother, Henderson passed the early part of his life : she taught him to read, pointed out the proper authors, and induced him to imprint upon his memory and recite select passages from Shakespeare, Pope, Addison, or any other English classic in her possession; his biographer states, that the wonder-working magic of the old bard enchanted his imagination, opened a new creation to his fancy, and prompted him to enquire how those characters were represented which afforded him so much delight in the perusal.   The description promoted a most eager wish to see a play : a wish which could not then be gratified, for in Newport it is said there were in those days no players.*   Learning and reciting speeches

* This cannot be strictly true, as players occasionally visited the town during the last century : amongst their number was Mr. Roger Kemble's Company.

improved a memory naturally tenacious, and gave him an early relish for 'polite literature, by this his taste was formed, and he frequently declared that by this he acquired what knowledge he had of the English language, for of the rules of grammar he was totally ignorant; and to his latest day Mr. Henderson not only always spoke of his mother's attention with filial gratitude, but when his situation enabled him to follow the impulse of his mind he made her happiness his first care, and the fond mother lived to see her instructions matured by time, and the public distinguish and protect what she had planted and fostered.

The following instance shews in what manner Mrs. Henderson was regarded by her two sons: when the eldest was ten, and John but eight years old, Mrs. Henderson was afflicted with a violent nervous disorder, which ended in melancholy; and while thus suffering, she one morning left her house, and sons, who awaited her return with impatience; night approached, but their mother did not come, and full of terrors the two boys went in search of her: ignorant what course to take, they wandered until midnight about the places where she used to walk; wandering without success they agreed to return home, but neither of them knew the way. Fatigued, alarmed, and distressed, they sat down on a bank to weep, when they observed at some distance a luminous appearance, and supposing it to be a candle in some friendly habitation they hastily directed their steps towards it: but as they moved, the light moved also, and glided from field to field for a considerable time; at length it seemed fixed, and on their near approach vanished on the side of a large piece of water: on the margin they found their mother asleep, from which she was roused by the presence and tears of her children. In after life, and while in his full career of success, Henderson often asserted, that he believed the light to be neither an ignis fatuus, nor a creation of the imagination, but a kind interposition of Providence for the preservation of the widow and the widow's sons.

At the age of eleven John Henderson was sent to a school at Hemel Hempstead, where he remained above twelve months, and was then placed under Mr. Fournier, a drawing master; in this situation he met with very ill treatment, and in about a year left the place to reside with his uncle, Mr. Cripps, a Working Silversmith in Saint James's, and his mother's intention was that he should learn the trade, but the death of Mr. Cripps put an end to that scheme. When about twenty years of age, Henderson was left with few connections, and without any determinate pursuit; he was accordingly advised to turn his attention to the stage, for

which he was thought to be eminently qualified. John
Notwithstanding an incompacted form, and a Henderson.
voice deficient in a mellifluous silvery tone, the
strength of his judgment, and the fervency of his
mind, broke through the mounds which nature
seemed to have placed between him and excel-
lence.   He discriminated with peculiar pro-
priety, says his biographer Ireland, the melancholy Jaques and the pensive Hamlet, the whim-
sical Benedict and the voluptuous Falstaff.   In
the whole of the latter part he was without a
competitor.

While delivering public recitations at Free-
mason's Hall, his friend, Mr. Sharpe, happening
to make Henderson acquainted with Cowper's
John Gilpin, then lately published, proposed that
he should recite it, though Mr. Sharpe admitted
that he did not anticipate the prodigious effect of
that story when the public attention was directed
to it.   These readings were only continued during
the Lent of 1785, and yet the profit amounted to
the extraordinary sum of eight hundred pounds.
One evening, while descending from his desk, a
person wriggled up to him and said, Pray who did
teach you to read Mr. Henderson ?   My mother
Sir, was the laconic reply.

Southey, in his life of Cowper, says, that a
gentleman who was present at one of the recitations informed him, that when the tale of John
Gilpin was read, " the whole audience chuckled ;

and Mrs. Siddons, who sat next to me, lifted her unequalled dramatic hands, and clapped as heartily as she herself used to be applauded in the same manner."

Mr. Henderson, occasionally on his visits to his friends at Newport Pagnell, delivered public recitations at the Swan Inn, and until his death he kept up a correspondence with Mr. George Pitt Hurst, a Solicitor of this town. Mr. Henderson died on the 25th of November of this same year, in the 40th year of his age ; and on the third of December was buried in Westminster Abbey, near Doctor Johnson and David Garrick, the Chapter and the Choir attending to pay respect to his memory : the pall was supported by the Honourable Mr. Byng, Mr. Malone, Mr. Whiteford, Mr. Stevens, and Mr. Hoole.

Mrs. Henderson died at Newport Pagnell, having survived her son for many years; her eldest son, a youth of great promise, died in a decline.

The Poet Cowper.

The poet Cowper, in a letter addressed to Lady Hesketh, dated 3rd June, 1788, enquires whether she had ever seen an advertisement by one Fowle, a dancing master of Newport Pagnell : his name however was Towle, and he attended here once a week. The Poet says, " The advertisement is the most extravagantly ludicrous affair of the kind I ever saw. The author of it had the good hap to be crazed, or he would never have

produced anything half so clever, for you will ever Christopher
observe that they who are said to have lost their Towle.
wits have more than other people ; it is therefore
only a slander with which envy prompts the
malignity of persons in their senses to asperse
wittier than themselves.   There are countries
in the world where the mad have justice done
them : where they are revered as the subjects
of inspiration, and consulted as oracles; poor
Fowle would have made a figure there." The
advertisement was printed by the well-known
Benjamin Leverett, of Newport Pagnell, and is
as follows :—

AT Mr. CHRISTOPHER TOWLES, in High-Street,
in COVENTRY, and at Miss TOWLES, in Penny-
farthing-Street, in Oxford.   YOUNG LADIES are gen-
teely Borded, and Taught all Manner of NEEDLE-WORK,
SPELLING and READING, at 12l. 12s. per Year, Entrance
1l. 1s. MUSIC, DANCING, WRITING, FRENCH, and DRAW-
ING, at usual Prices, to be paid for separately; to Teach
which, proper Persons will be Employ'd.—Mr. and Miss
TOWLES, assures the Gentlemen and Ladies, who please
to honour them with the care of their Daughters, that the
strictest Attention will be paid to the Improvement of the
Morals and Behaviour of the Young Ladies committed to
their care; and ev'ry Method taken to render their Schooles
a Scene of Pleasure and Improvement.—The Holidays are
Christmas and Midsummer, a Month each.—Mr. TOWLE,
Teaches all Sorts of ENGLISH, FRENCH, ITALIAN, and
FLEMISH, Slow and Quick DANCES; to complete all
Persons to be Performers in Operas, Playhouses, Saddlers-
Wells, Balls, Assemblies, &c.--The English Dances that

he Teaches is, ten Thousand times preferable to all the Foreign-Dances, Rounds, Hornpipes, Cottillions, and Figure Dances, which is also of the greatest use in the ARMY and NAVY, the SINGLE-STICK, QUARTER-STAFF, BROAD-SWORD, SMALL-SWORD, WRESTLING, BOXING, RUNNING, JUMPING, SWIMMING, RINGING, and HORSE-MANSHIP of all Sorts, PAINTING, DRAWING, STAGE-PLAYERS of all Sorts, Music, SURGERY, in ev'ry Circumstance of Fraction and Dislocation, &c.

He will be Answerable that a Young Gentleman beginning to dance at about 12 Years of Age, and continueing for the Space of three Years a regular Scholar to him, if he is design'd for a Soldier, &c. in Twelve Monthes Time. he will understand the Firelock, &c. Sword, &c. and every Menevre better than many who have been 12 Years in the ARMY, and he will prepare a Person that must go to SEA, to understand the Use of the Sails upon any Sort of VESSEL, beginning at a Scull or Oar, up to a First Rate Man of War, also better than some that have been 20 Years for the Land Service; he requires 4, 6, 8, 10, or 12, of and for a constant for 12, 18, or 24, Monthes two Days in each Fortnight, &c. his Price for Teaching for the Land or Sea-Service, is Entrance each Scholar, 1l. 1s. the Quarter 1l. 1s. he also Teaches on 20 different INSTRUMENTS of MUSIC, also Tunes, Strings, or Quils, HARPSICHORDS, SPINETS, and VIRGINALS; Strings GUITARS, DULCIMERS, BELL-HARPS, and VIOLINS, &c. the Price he Teaches Young Gentlemen that are not design'd either for the Land or Sea-Service, and Young Ladies in their Families, is according as he gives attendance.

Mr. TOWLE, undertakes CONCERTS, BALLS, and ASSEMBLIES, and Assisteth at any undertaken by any other Person, either Public or Private, he proposes to have a DANCE one night in Each Month, for the Grown Gentlemen and Ladies, and a Public Day for his Scholars

at the Half-Years End, and a Public Ball at the Years-
End in every Town he Teaches in.

ENTRANCE, 10s. 6d. his Price for Teaching per Quarter, One Day in each Fortnight, 10s. 6d.

Two Days in ditto, 1l. 1s. three Days in Ditto, 1l. 11s.
6d. four Days in Ditto, 2l. 2s.

Each Scholar for the Ball, 3s. each ditto, at Public
Day, 1s. 6d. each Person paying Evening Dance, 1s.

Attendance on Gentlemens Families, Entrance each
Scholar, 1l. 1s. each Journey he goes 10s. 6d. Entrance
of all Sorts, to be paid at the Time of beginning ; Quarters
to be paid at the End, each journey to be paid, &c.
Public Days and Evening Dances, to be paid as they enter
into the Room.

There are Dancing Masters in London, and many other
parts of England, Scotland, Ireland, and Wales, &c. who
gives attendance on their Schools once a day, one day in
each week, either in the morning part of the day, or the
evening part, &c. and others that gives attendance both
morning and afternoon, one day in each week, some who
gives attendance two days in each fortnight, &c. &c. and
to thousands of persons that are not acquainted with my
method of teaching, they will naturely think that my giving
attendance only one day in each fortnight, that it is an im-
possibility to bring my scholars to any sort of good knowledge or performances, in five years time, to answer all that
any one or any of them can or will or doth or may or shall
hereafter say, I have and I can and I will teach, if I only
give attendance one day in each fortnight, (that is) two
hours in the morning, and three hours in the afternoon, I
will make a scholar or my scholars to understand the
theare and practical parts of Dancing, &c. better in 12
months than all or any can or hath in 36 months, for any
wager they will.

x

Christopher Towle.

☞ No man can be well prepared in any sort of genteel trades, professions, sicances, employments, servitudes, music, the army, or navy, unless they can dance exceeding well; dancing will make a man stand and walk, and look, and speak well; to be courteous, and civil, obliging, and complaisant, and genteel, and of a fine forgiving merciful disposition; which all will be soon attained with all persons who learn to dance very well, I have known and heard of persons who has been good Dancers, to advance themselves from a quirister to a bishop, from a private man to a general, from a cabin boy to a admiral, from a lawyer clerk to a counsellor, and from that to a judge, from a clerk to a merchant, to be a merchant himself; and ten thousand circumstances of the same kind might be enumerated, &c. &c. Dancing gives a person a easy looking and speaking, to his superiors and inferiors, it takes off those slow and effeminately proud deluding look, that some of the sectary make use of, to a most abominable and reached disgraced degree, and quite despisable to every honest man, whilst the good natured Dancer, &c. behaves with the very strictest part of modesty, and a easy obliging behaviour to all and all sorts of people of all denominations; if I was to enumerate the great use that Dancing is of to women in all sorts of trades and employments, and all sorts of services, in all respects beginning with one of the Maids of Honour to the Queen, and go through all sorts and degrees of quality and gentry, &c. &c. and trades, &c. it would be a very great task, &c. in short, Dancing is the very greatest support to trades and manufactures of all sorts, and professions of every kind that can be mentioned, and all those sort of persons who has anything to say against Dancing are enemies to the whole community, &c. All free schooles, charity schooles, and persons who desire to promote Improvements for either boys or girls, should leave a very good *salary* for a Dancing Master, to instruct children for ever, &c., this I recommend to all the whole community of all nations, kingdoms, and all the inhabitants upon the face of the whole earth. Christopher
Towle.

Signed by me,

CHRISTOPHER TOWLE.

His presant Schooles is in 1783; In Oxford: Coventry Northampton Daventry Hooburn Newport Pagnell: Wellingborough: Wolston and Hill.

The beautiful words of the Poet

" That tears by bards and heroes shed,

" Alike immortalize the dead.

are strikingly illustrated in the case of a young gentleman of this town, Mr. Thomas Abbot Hamilton, whose tomb is in our Church-yard; and perchance, years after it has fallen into decay, there will be thousands to whom Mr. Hamilton's name will be familiar, from the inscription with which the muse of Cowper has adorned his tomb:

Beneath this Stone are deposited the Remains of

Thos. Abbot Hamilton,

Who departed this Life July 7th, 1788,

In the 32nd Year of his Age.

Pause here and think, a monitory rhyme
Demands one moment of thy fleeting time;
Consult life's silent clock, thy bounding vein:
Seems it to say health here has long to reign.
Hast thou the vigour of thy youth? an eye
That beams delight? a heart untaught to sigh?

Yet fear : Youth, ofttimes healthful and at ease,
Anticipates a day it never sees ;
And many a Tomb like Hamilton's, aloud
Exclaims prepare thee for an early shroud.

W. COWPER.

Rev. Saml. Greatheed.

Mr. Hamilton was brother to the lady of the Reverend Samuel Greatheed Cowper wrote this inscription at the request of Mr. Greatheed, whose intimate friend he was, and of whom he speaks in terms of regard and esteem, and describes him as a man of letters and of taste.   Mr. Greatheed was originally an Assistant Military Engineer : but afterwards, being desirous of entering the Christian Ministry, amongst the Dissenters, he came to Newport Pagnell to be educated for that purpose, under the care of Mr. Bull ; in 1786, having completed his studies, Mr. Greatheed rendered that gentleman important service as an assistant in his duties as Tutor of the Academy.   During his residence here he married the daughter of Mr. Hamilton, of this town ; he was for some time Minister of the Independent Chapel at Woburn : but many years before his death he removed to a distant part of the country, and died about twenty years ago at an advanced age.

Mrs. Dalway.

Mrs. Dalway, who resided at Newport Pagnell after her husband's death, died in 1789, and on the 12th of August was buried at Lathbury ; she had two children, but her son dying unmarried, her daughter became entitled to her mother's moiety of the Lathbury estate.

In the year 1794, the Port Field was enclosed by Act of Parliament: the tythes were not affected by the enclosure, but power was given to persons entitled to them to take a compensation, either in land or otherwise. On the 18th of November in the following year, an earthquake, which was felt in various places from York to Bristol, affected Newport Pagnell, the concussion being felt by many of the inhabitants: and at the Neptune Public-house the bells were set gingling, to the alarm and consternation of the family. *Port Field A. D. 1794.*

Mr. William Underwood, of this parish, who died in the year 1798, bequeathed the sum of ten pounds, to be annually laid out in bread, and distributed on New Year's Day, for ever. A few years before, Mr. James Leverett, Surgeon, of Witney, in Oxfordshire, had also given three hundred pounds, the interest to be laid out in bread, and distributed amongst the poor every Sunday, for ever. *Mr. Wm. Underwood. Mr. James Leverett.*

On the 30th of April, in the year 1799, died Miss Jane, usually called Madam Symes, the last of the second house of the Andrewes's, at Lathbury, and on the 8th of May was buried at that Church. This lady, like her mother, kept her town house; and while there in 1780, during the persecution of the Roman Catholics, by the followers *Miss Symes. A. D. 1799.*

Miss Symes of Lord George Gordon, she was exposed to great peril through having a servant in her house of that persuasion, a fact it seems of which Miss Symes was unacquainted. It was generally expected that Miss Symes's property would have passed to the Andrewes's; but there is a tradition that Mrs. Symes conjured her daughter not to let her property pass to any member of that family, and that Miss Symes had bequeathed by her will her entire property to charitable purposes; Miss Symes however abandoned that design, and on her death Mansel Dawkin Mansel, Esquire, became possessed of her property. Mr. Mansel was an active country gentleman, and survived his generous friend and benefactress more than twenty years: since his death the estate and mansion at Lathbury have become the property of Lord Hood.

Bridges.
A. D. 1810.

Canal.

In the year 1810, the thoroughfare through this town was greatly improved by the re-erection of the bridges at North-end and Tickford, and widening and improving the approaches; about which period an Act of Parliament was obtained for cutting a Canal from Newport to join the Grand Junction Canal at Great Linford; this Canal has proved of great service to the corn and coal trade of the town, it was designed to be continued to Bedford, but the plan was not carried into execution, and from the altered state of the times it is not now likely to be done:

about the same time also an Act of Parliament Bedford
was obtained, for improving the road from Road.
Newport to Bedford.

Having proceeded thus far with our history, we
will now state some facts of a descriptive, rather
than an historical nature, and the first which
claims our notice is

THE CHURCH.

It is a plain Gothic building, dedicated to The Church.
St. Peter and St. Paul, and a few years ago was
greatly enlarged and improved, at an expense of
nearly seven thousand pounds. It consists of a
tower, nave, two side aisles, two side galleries,
organ loft, and chancel; in the tower there are
eight bells, bearing the following inscriptions:—

1st.   At proper times my voice I'll raise,   The Bells.
         And sound to my subscribers' praise.
                 T. Lester, fecit, 1749.
2nd and 5th.   T. Lester, 1749.
3rd.   John Purratt, and John Smith, Churchwardens.
Lester and Pack, London, fecit, 1769.
4th.   T. Lester, 1749.   Robert Perrott.   Philomusicus
Auditu Dignus.
6th.   Thomas Lester made me, 1749.
7th and 8th.   The Revd. Charles Kipling, Vicar, William
White, and Edward Cleaver, Churchwardens.   T. Mears,
London, fecit, 1816.

The Eighth Bell was merely re-cast, and the
ancient inscription has been preserved:

Nuntia sum Captæ Perituræ Previa Vitæ
Et Modo Transactæ Vox Ego Certa Tuæ.

The Church. The interior of the Church is very handsome ; it is well pewed, and contains a great many free seats. The font is modern ; in the south aisle are three stone stalls ; the cloth on the altar is marked N. P. 1664, and the altar piece contains the Ten Commandments, the Belief, and the Lord's Prayer. In addition to the inscriptions on the monuments, given in the text, are the following :

CHANCEL.

Church
Monuments.

In the Vault beneath lie the Remains of
Sarah Needham, Daughter of Caroline and the
Revd. C. Kipling, Vicar of this Parish,
Who Died April 9th, 1813, Aged 1 Year and 5 Months.

———

Sacred to the Memory of
Henry Van Hagen, Esquire, of Tickford Park,
in this Parish,
Who Departed this Life 18th June, 1832, Aged 40.
"As for me I will behold thy face in righteousness ; I shall be satisfied when I awake with thy likeness." Ps. 17.

———

Thomas Pike Died July 10th, 1831,
Aged 60 Years.

Ann Price, Wife of Luke Price,
Died January 30th, 1837,
Aged 31 Years.

———

J. G. Durham, A.M., Vicar of this Parish,
Died June 7, 1832,
Aged 50.

SOUTH AISLE.

Here lyeth the Body of Thomas Jenkins,
Who Departed this Life June the 13, 1705,
and Mary his Wife.

William Lucas Died 29th Dec. 1827, Aged 69.
Letitia, his Wife, Died 31st Aug. 1823, Aged 59.

Under this Place lieth y° Body of
Thomas Taylor, who Departed this Life August y° 12th,
1719, in the 47th Year of his Age.

Also y° Body of
Thomas Taylor, the Son of Thomas and Ann Taylor,
Who Departed this Life April the 16th, 1719,
In the 4th Year of his Age.

Under this Place lieth y° Body of Mr. Chapman Taylor,
Who Departed this Life
September the 30th, 1705, in the 17th Year of his Age.

Also y° Body of his Sister, Mrs. Rebekah Taylor,
Who Departed this Life August y° 21th, 1706.

Dorothea Conjux Dilectissima
Johannis Hurst Generosi
E Vita Excessit vicessimo
secundo Die Octobris
Anno Salutis 1749. Ætatis 37.
In Eodem Tumulo Etiam Hic Requiescit
Foelicem Expectans Resurrectionem,
Johannes Hurst Maritus Ejus Amantissimus.
Qui Decessit die Octobris Quarto,
Anno Dom¹ MDCCLXXII.
Ætatis Suæ LXVI.

Y

Georgius Pitt Hurst Generosus.
Filius Natu Maximus,
Johannis et Dorotheæ,
Obiit die Martis Decimo Nono,
MDCCCXVII.
Ætatis Suæ 73.

———

Here ly Interred yᵉ severall Bodys of
Roger Chapman, Esqr.
Rebecca, his Wife, and
Felicia, their Daughter,
Who Dyed on the Days and in the Yeares underwritten.

Rebecca Dyed yᵉ 25ᵉ of Apr. 1697.
Felicia, who was Married to Capt. Ja: DVMAS,
Dyed yᵉ 31ᵒ of Decbr, 1698,
And Roger Dyed yᵉ 15ᵉ of Febr. 1702.

———

Hic Requiescit.
Felicem Expectans Resurrectionem
Joannes Rogers Generosus
Vixit Annos LXXV.
Decessit die Jan. XXVII.
Anno Dom. MDCCXXVI.

———

Here Resteth the Body of James Hartley,
Who departed this Life June the 27th, 1666, Aged 63.

———

Here lyeth yᵉ Body of
Alice, yᵉ Wife of Mr. John Chowne,
Who departed this life March yᵉ 21, $\frac{1699,}{700,}$
In yᵉ 46 year of her Age.
Here also lyeth yᵉ Body of
Mr. John Chowne,
Who departed this life May yᵉ — —

Thomas Forster died 23 Jan, 1775, Aged 56.
Thomas Godfrey Forster, (Son of Thomas Forster)
died 30 Jan. 1792, Aged 43.

Thomas Barringer, Son of Thomas and Ann Barringer,
Late of Ravenstone,
died February 2, 1810, Aged 45,
Sarah Barringer, Wife of Samuel Barringer,
died January 4, 1825, Aged 76,
Samuel Barringer, Husband of Sarah Barringer,
died December 27, 1833, Aged 76.

Mary Knibb, died 2 Jan. 1822, Aged 78.
George Valentine Knibb, died 5th Jan. 1817, Aged 37.
Mary Ann Knibb, died 12 July, 1824, Aged 43.
George Knibb died 23rd Octr. 1826, Aged 76.

Hic Iacet Thomæ Pvlford,
In Artibvs Bach
Obijt 29 Maij, 1672, Ætat svæ 21.
Ante Obitvm Nemo.

John Perrott, Son of Richard and Mary Perrott.
1721.

Beneath this Stone are deposited the Remains of
Ann Plowman, Daughter of Thomas Foster, Senr.
Was born Septr. 27, 1753.
Died June 1st, 1840,

Here lyeth yᵉ Body of Thomas Bazeley,
of Hemingforth Abbott, in yᵉ County of Huntingdon,
Yeoman,
Who dyed yᵉ 4th of October, 1703,
In the 63rd year of his Age,

Robert Collison,
Died 8th March, 1803, Aged 54.
Lucy Collison,
Died 24th August, 1799, Aged 50.

Mr. Samuel White,
Died October ye 11, 1701.

NORTH AISLE.

Here lieth ye Body of
Frances Mander, Wife of Daniel Mander,
Who departed this Life Octr. the 24th, 1704,
In the 26th year of her Age.

Here lieth the Body of Susannah Kilpin,
Who departed this Life December 6th, 1711, Aged 71.
Here I lie, sleeping in the dust,
Untill the resurrection of the just :
Untill our Christ (Saviour) does say,
Arise, ye dead, and come away.

Here lieth the Body of Mr. John Johnson,
He departed this Life the 28th of August, 1711,
In the 48th year of his Age.
Read on the other hand, and thou shalt see,
The dismal tokens of mortality :
Here lies the Mother, with her Children dear;
And here the Father, coming in the rear ;
All sleeping now together in the dust
Untill the resurrection of the just.

Here lieth the Body of Mary Johnson,
Wife of John Johnson, and their 12 Children,

She died October 10th, 1708,
In the 35 year of her Age.
What root and branches too ! O cruel death,
So early in our day to stop our breath !
Tis true we all lye conquered here by thee,
Yet thou, O death, soon conquered must be ;
When thou thy sleeping prisoners must let go,
Free from the feares of any after blow.

NAVE.

Here lyeth the Body of Samuel Christie, Esq.
Who died the 21st of July, 1703.
Here also lyeth the Body of Ann, his Wife,
Who died August the 28th, 1713.

To the Memory of William Pomfret,
Late of this Parish, Gent.
Who, together with his three Wives, and a numerous
Offspring,
Lyeth near this place Interred.
He departed this Life the 6th day of June, 1666,
Virtus post Funera Vivit.

Here lieth ye Body of Mr. George Chapman,
Who departed this Life March ye 1, 1696,
Ætate sve 70.

There are in different parts of the Church
several old stones, robbed of their brasses, which
are probably some of those to which Browne
Willis refers. Besides those already mentioned
there are no monuments in the Church-yard that
particularly claim our attention. The Church-

yard is in an airy open situation; and the view from the iron railings, at the end of the terrace, is one of the finest landscapes in the neighbourhood.

VICARS.—Revd. Robert Watson, deceased,   1783

—— William Davies, ditto   1809

—— Charles Kipling, removed,   1823

—— William Marshall, ditto   1831

—— James George Durham, deceased, 1832

—— George Morley

THE INDEPENDENT CHAPEL

Is a large brick building, in a retired situation; it is well pewed, and will hold about eight hundred people. A brass plate on the reading board of the pulpit in the vestry contains the following inscription :—

"This board once formed a part of the pulpit of the celebrated John Bunyan, and was presented to the Trustees of the Independent Meeting by the

REVD. WILLIAM BULL.

'Revere the man whose Pilgrim marks the road,
And guides the progress of the soul to God.'

COWPER."

The burial ground is a very quiet, beautiful spot, and is planted with various shrubs and flowers. There are vaults under the vestry and chapel : a school over the vestry, by a sliding partition, forms part of the Chapel. A monument to the memory of the Beaty family is from the chisel of Bacon ; the inscriptions on the monuments in the Chapel are as follow :—

In Memory of Thomas Hacket,
Late of Oakley, Bedfordshire.
Formerly a Student in the Newport Pagnell
Evangelical Institution,
Who having nearly completed his Studies was suddenly
removed to a better world,
June IV, MDCCCXXI, Aged 27 years.
His Remains were Interred in the adjoining Burial Ground.

Chapel
Monuments.

In Memory of the Revd. Thomas James,
Eldest Son of Mr. James,
Of Clarbeston, in Pembrokeshire.
Who departed this life the 23rd of February, 1795,
In the 20th year of his Age,
While pursuing his Studies for the Ministry under the
Rev'd. William Bull.
His Remains were Interred in the adjoining burying ground.
O Reader !
Whatsoever thy hand findeth to do,
Do it with all thy might.

In Memory of Joseph Cripps,
Who departed this Life January 17th, 1827,
In the 68th year of his Age.
Susanna, his Wife,
Who died April 10th, 1839,
Aged 71 years, and
Mary, their Daughter,
Who died February 22nd, 1834,
In her 30th year.
" These all died in faith,"
Having, as Members of the Church of Christ in this place,
" Witnessed a good confession,"
and
"Adorned the doctrine of God their Saviour in all things."

This Tablet was erected A. D. 1829,

By the Congregation under the Pastoral care of the Revd

T. P. Bull,

To. perpetuate the Memory of

The Revd. John Gibbs,

Formerly of the University of Cambridge,

Who preached the Gospel in this town upwards of fifty-one Years. During twelve of which he was Vicar of this parish. Ejected from the Church, A. D. 1660, for conscientiously refusing to allow of promiscuous Communion at the Lord's Table. He retired with many of his congregation to a building near this spot, and continued his labours among them to the end of his days, except when interrupted by the Persecution and Imprisonment he endured for conscience sake. His valuable life, which was distinguished for Piety, Learning, and Usefulness, was closed on the 16th June, A. D. 1699, in the 72nd year of his Age.

His Remains were Interred near the South door of the Chancel, in the Church-yard of this Town.

Since that period it has pleased the great Head of the Church to continue in this place a succession of faithful Ministers, who have uniformly maintained those important doctrines which Mr. Gibbs preached, and for which he suffered. He was succeeded by the Revd. Thos. Tingey in 1699, John Hunt 1709, Wm. Hunt 1725, Humphrey Gainsborough 1743, — Affleck 1747, David Fordyce, A. M. 17.., James Belsham 1749, Wm. Bull, 1763.

Holiness becometh thine House,

O Lord, for ever.

This Tablet is sacred to the Memory of the late
Revd. Joseph Ward.
He was born at Market Lavington, Wilts,
the 2nd of January, 1771,
Became a resident at Newport Pagnell, A. D. 1803,
Was appointed a Deacon of the Christian Church
Assembling in this place A. D. 1824,
Died on the 2nd of June, 1829, Aged 58 Years.

" Remember his work of faith, and labour of love,
And patience of hope in the Lord Jesus Christ."

8 Thess. 1. 3.

————

I shall be satisfied when I awake with thy likeness.

17 Psal. 15 ver.

In the adjoining burying ground
Rest in lively hope the mortal Remains of
Elizabeth, Wife of William Barker Kilpin.
She was born at Stansted, Essex, 11th October, 1780,
Was united to this Christian Society 1st October, 1803,
Died 15th January, 1808,
After an illness of three days.
How many fall as sudden, not as safe.

Near the same spot lie interred two of their Children,
William Johnstone, and
Edward Wells Kilpin,
Who died in their Infancy.

————

Sacred to the Memory of
Amelia Ann Higgins,
Eldest Daughter of Walter and Ann Beaty,
Who departed this Life the 3rd of December, 1834,
Aged 76 Years.

" My flesh also shall rest in hope."—XVI Psalm, 9 ver.

z

Sacred to the Memory of most revered Parents,
Walter Beaty,
Who died on the 22nd May, 1791, aged 63,
and Ann Beaty,
Who died on the 24th November, 1799, aged 61,
and a beloved Brother,
Walter Beaty,
Who departed this Life 2nd December, 1801, aged 44,
This Marble is erected.

Sincere and just, beneficent and kind,
The friend, the Christian, in the *Father* joined.
The *Mother's* mildness blest each varying scene;
Her judgment just—her piety serene.
Their mingled worth adorned their Son's career,
And all who knew bemoaned our *Brother's* bier:
Beside their Urn fond Memory weeping stands,
While Faith unfolds to Hope the " House
not made with Hands."

———

Near this Monumental Tablet are deposited
the Remains of
Ann, Daughter of John and Sarah Hamilton,
of this Town,
and Wife of Samuel Greatheed.
She was born 27 March, 1758,
Became a Member of the Independent Church
Assembling in this place
7 March, 1784,
Departed this Life 28 August, 1807,
And was Interred 3rd September,

On the same day and hour, in which 19 years before she
had been married.

Reader, reflect a moment! One lies here,
Whose hope was humble, and whose heart sincere.

God gave her wealth—she lavished not the store,
Devoted to the duties of a Wife,
She scorned the gaudy vanities of life.
Her Husband much she loved—but more her God,
Meekly she bowed to his parental rod ;
And when by faith and patience purified,
She slept in Christ—'twas the Surviver died.

The Inscription on the Monument to the Memory of the Revd. William Bull is surmounted with a Medallion Portrait, before which is an open volume, bearing the following passage :

" Having made peace thro' the blood of his Cross."

Col. 1. 20.

Beneath this Tablet are deposited the Remains of
The Reverend William Bull,
Who was Ordained Pastor of the Church assembling in
this place, Octr. 11, 1764,
And gently breathed his Soul to Rest July 23, 1814,
In his 76th year.

To him, his friend the immortal Cowper, bears this
testimony :—

" He was a Dissenter, a liberal one, a man of letters and genius, master of a fine imagination, a man of erudition and ability."

These Talents he happily employed
In preaching JESUS CHRIST, and him crucified ;
And in training up young men for the Gospel Ministry.

His Church and Congregation
Thankful for the faithful and successful labors of half
a Century,
Have erected this small tribute of their gratitude & affection.

Near the same spot are also deposited
All that was mortal of Hannah Bull, wife of the Revd.
William Bull,

She fell asleep in Jesus, February 26, 1804, Aged 67 years.

Mrs.
Higgins's
Charity.

Mrs. Higgins, who died in 1834, bequeathed the sum of Twenty-five Pounds, to be distributed yearly for ever: Five Pounds to the Minister of the Independent Chapel for the time being, and Twenty Pounds amongst the poor persons belonging to the Congregation, to be expended in Bread and Coals—one-half part on Christmas Day, and the other half on New Year's Day.

Dissenters'
Academy.

The Dissenters, in connection with the Chapel, have an Academy here for the Education of Young Men for the Christian Ministry: it was established in 1780, by the united efforts of the well-known Revd. John Newton, of Olney, the Poet Cowper, the Revd. John Clayton, Senr., Mr. John Thornton, and others. Mr. Bull was appointed Tutor, who, as we have already stated, was in 1786 assisted by Mr. Greatheed. Mr. Thornton was so interested in the success of this useful Institution, that a short time after its commencement he took the entire charge of its maintenance upon himself until the death of the late Mr. Bull, in 1814: since that time the Academy has been supported by voluntary contributions. In the year 1800 the Revd. Thomas Palmer Bull was appointed Co-Pastor with his father at the Chapel, and Assistant Tutor in the Academy; and thirty-three years afterwards this gentleman had the same assistance rendered him, in his duties as Pastor and Tutor, in the person of his son, the Revd. Josiah Bull, A. M. In the month of October of this year (1842), Mr. Bull and his Son resigned their connection with the Academy, when the Revd. John Watson became the sole Tutor. The average number of Students in the house is eight, who continue their studies four years.

The PARTICULAR BAPTISTS have a small Baptist Chapel here. In Thompson's List of Particular Chapel. Baptist Churches it is stated that the Church was formed in the year 1662: the Chapel contains, amongst others, a Monument to the memory of Mr. Thomas Eaglestone, who died in the year 1800, and who left a liberal endowment for the support of the Chapel. The present Minister is the Revd. Robert Abbott, who was settled here on the 1st of August, 1840.

The WESLEYAN METHODISTS' Chapel is a plain Wesleyan brick building, erected in 1815, and will hold Chapel. about three hundred people.

SCHOOLS.—There are, besides Dr. Atterbury's Schools. School, the National School, the Royal British School, the Girls' and Infant Schools, a Sewing School held twice a week at the National School, a Girls' School in Tickford-end, supported by the liberality of Mrs. Van Hagen, besides Sunday Schools belonging to the various congregations.

Fairs and Markets.

FAIRS AND MARKETS.—The Market is on a Saturday, and in the Winter of 1841 a Corn and Stock Market was established on Wednesdays. The Fairs are February 22, March 21, April 22, June 22, August 29, October 22, and December 22.

Pillow Lace.

The only article of manufacture carried on in the Town is that of Bobbin, or Pillow Lace. About thirty years ago a good Lace-maker could earn two shillings a day; but now, through the introduction of Machine Lace, the value of the Pillow Lace is reduced more than fifty per cent.

The Town.

The Town consists of three principal streets : the High Street, from the North Bridges to the entrance of the Town, S. W. from the Wolverton Station of the London and Birmingham Railway ; Saint John Street, branching off at the Cannon Corner, through Tickford End, being the original London Road ; and Silver Street, leading from Saint John Street to Marsh End. The parts of Newport called the Green, Marsh End, and Tickford End, laying very low, are subject to inundations during the Winter floods ; and it is reported, that in the Saracen's Head Yard, which is the highest part of the town, on the 5th of October, 1570, during a violent tempest that happened throughout the kingdom, a remarkable inundation proceeded from a spring ; at the same time two houses were thrown down by the shock, and a man and woman crushed to death by their fall.

Newport Pagnell, in the diocese of Lincoln, and deanery of Newport Pagnell, is in the northern part of the County of Bucks., and is distant from London fifty miles, four from the Wolverton Railway Station, five from Olney, fifteen from Northampton, six from Stony Stratford, fourteen from Buckingham, six from Fenny Stratford, nine from Woburn, and thirteen from Bedford. *Ecclesiastical Division.* *Distance from other Towns.*

Newport Pagnell, being a Post and Posting Town in the principal North-West Road, was at one time a celebrated thoroughfare ; the Grand Junction Canal, and subsequently the London and Birmingham Railway, have in a great measure taken off the Waggons and Coaches which passed through Newport. A correspondent from this Town, Neoportensis, in the Gentleman's Magazine, 1821, says, " That it would be a curiosity of no small interest, if, among local vestiges, the Historian of a Post Town were able to enumerate what persons of importance have changed horses," and he quotes a letter written at Newport in 1711, by Mr. Richard Grinnett, the travelling companion of Sir John and Lady Guise, which appears in " The Honourable Loves," the correspondence *A celebrated thoroughfare.*

(under the fictitious names of Pylades and Co-rinna), of Mr. Grinnett and Mrs. Elizabeth Thomas, of Great Russell Street, Bloomsbury, celebrated in the '*Dunciad*'; and one hundred years after this, Lord Byron stopped at the Swan Hotel, on his journey into Nottinghamshire, on account of his Mother's illness; having, while resting here, received intelligence of her death, he addressed a letter from hence; in lamenting her death, he adopts the beautiful sentiment of Gray, " that we can only have one Mother."

Races.

Cricket Club.

Reading Room.

Charities.

Races existed here as early as 1720; in 1828 they were re-established, but after a few years again fell into disuse. A Cricket Club, established in 1819, is well attended on every Tuesday throughout the months of June, July, and August: the Club consists of many of the nobility and gentry in the neighbourhood of Newport Pagnell, and the adjoining counties. There is a public News and Reading Room supported by the Clergy and Gentry in the neighbourhood, and there are also connected with the Town two or three well-conducted Book Societies. The Newport and Olney Troops of the Bucks. Yeomanry, commanded by Captain George Lucas, assemble in Bury-field, for their annual training.

In addition to the Charities already referred to, there are White and Waller's Charities; the Feoffees have the management of the funds

derived from Kitchell's or Kitchen's Dole, Child's
Gift, Holiday's Gifts, Holiday's Closes, Read,
Hobbs, and Cropthorn's Gifts, Sybley's Gift, the
Four Almshouses on the Green, Gift for the
Relief of the Poor, and the Amendment of the
Church, Highways, and Bridges ; Sweetmore
Holme, Blood's Gift, Godstowe's Gift, and Back-
yard of Saracen's Head Inn ; producing, ac-
cording to the Report of the Charity Commis-
sioners, an annual income of about One Hundred
Pounds.

Goodman's Charity is under the controul of Goodman's Charity.
the Master and Governors of Saint John's Hospital ; it consists of the Rent of a Close, about
Eight Pounds, in Little Crawley, which is payable to the Widow of any Vicar of the Parish ;
and in the absence of a Vicar's Widow, the same
is to be laid out for the putting forth of a poor
Child or Children of the Parish, Apprentice, the
Children of such Minister or Ministers being
first preferred.

In the Parliamentary Returns of 1786, an Acre Widows' Acre.
of Land is stated to have been given by an unknown Donor, for the use of Poor Widows of
Newport Pagnell, and to be then vested, in the
Overseers of the Poor, who sold always the
annual produce by Auction, and that it produced
then from Three Pounds Ten Shillings, to Five
Pounds. There are about three Acres of Land,
called as above, in Bury-Meadow, the limits of

which are ascertained by a ditch.   The herbage
of this Acre Field belongs to those who have
Rights of Common in Bury-Meadow, but the
Crop or produce of the Land is sold yearly, by
Auction, by the Overseers, about the first week
in July, and the proceeds of the Sale are given
away by them; amongst all the Widows of the
Parish who apply for a share on the succeeding
New Year's Day.   The produce of the Sale in
July, 1842, was £10. 15s.   The average num-
ber of Widows who make application is 80.

The
Antiquary
Martin.

Amongst the remarkable men, natives of Newport Pagnell, of whom we have been able to
obtain but little information, is the Antiquary
Martin, of whom Old Fuller speaks as his worthy
friend, a native of Newport Pagnell, at that time

Bishop
Harley

beneficed near Northampton.   Of Bishop Harley,
to whom we referred in Page 51, we find he was
one of those great and good men who helped
on the cause of the Reformation, by preaching
Anti-Papal Doctrines, and powerfully pressing
home to his hearers the Cardinal Doctrine of
Justification by Faith alone.

ADDENDA.

———

PAGE 18.—CHURCH BRASSES.—A Member of the Cambridge Camden Society, (who has paid great attention to the interesting subject of Church Brasses), is of opinion that the date of the Brass is about 1450.

PAGE 64.—ANDREWES.—The name of Andrewes first occurs in the Lathbury Register, 1594; but this Register beginning in 1547, from which there are extracts in the British Museum, is not now in existence. John Andrewes, father of the first Sir William, purchased the Manor of Lathbury of Mrs. Chester, Mrs. Newdigate, and Mrs. Hampden, (Grandmother of the Patriot), the three Co-heiresses of Mr. Anthony Cave—see Page 44. In Leland's Itinerary, 1549, Lathbury is said to be the property of "Old John Andrewes"; but antecedent to this, Richard Andrewes, of Chicheley, by his Will in 1521, desires to be buried at Lathbury, and gives a legacy to the repair of the Church.

PAGE 77.—Colonel Sir Samuel Luke's Banner.—Argent; a bugle horn Sable, stringed, Or; Crest, on a Wreath Argent and Sable, a Bull's Head, issuant and in profile, Azure, winged on the Shoulders or Neck, and Armed Or.

The Cornet or Flag of Colonel Sir Samuel Luke. Gules; in fess, and spread at the ends; a cord of Gold, variously twisted and turned, and having belike four ends, between which in two lines, in letters of Gold thus—in the first LEX a book, in pale and erect, closed and clasped of Gold, and then follows, SVPREMA; beneath the other thus SALVS, in an oval-like barrways, the City of London, and then follows, PATRIÆ; fringed Argent and Gules.

Page 115.—Written on the Grave of Mark Slingsby,
at Newport Pagnell, Sept. 3, 1810.—*Gents. Mag.* 1821.

> Stranger? with no unholy tread
> Pollute this mansion of the dead :
> Stranger! whoe'er thou art, draw near,
> Here may'st thou shed the sacred tear ;
> Whate'er thy name, whate'er thy fate,
> Thou ow'st a tribute to the great :
> If, reckless of our hero's fame,
> Thou stand'st unconscious of that claim ;
> If no ambition fires the blood,
> Thou ow'st a tribute to the good :
> And here, from all intrusion free,
> Pay the sweet meed of loyalty.
> Ask'st thou for whom these tears are shed ?
> Great Slingsby slumbers with the dead.

Page 122.—Tyringham.—In the year 1778 this estate
passed to William Praed, Esquire, by his marriage with
Elizabeth, the co-heiress, with her sister Sarah, of Bar-
naby Backwell, Esquire, the direct lineal descendant of
the Tyringhams and Backwells.   Mr. Praed was succeeded
by his Son, James Backwell Praed, Esquire, who was for
some time one of the Members of Parliament for the county;
on his death in 1837 he was succeeded by his Son, William
Backwell Praed, Esquire, a minor.   The original family
mansion was situated much nearer the church at Tyringham
than the present handsome modern erection.

Page 157.—Mr. Richard Uthwatt died in 1731, and
not 1749; he was buried at Lathbury on the 10th of
November.

Pages 169 and 180.—Mrs. Symes had the whole estate
at Lathbury for her life; her Sister, Mrs. Dalway, was
disinherited, having offended her father by her marriage,
and never had any interest in the Lathbury property.

INDEX.

LIST OF SUBSCRIBERS.

Abbott, Miss, Newport Pagnell
Adderley, Thomas, Esq., Upper Clapton
Adkins, Mr., Ravenstone Mills
Abel & Sons, Messrs., Northampton
Allbright, Mr., Newport Pagnell
Andrewes, Rev. W., Buckingham
Arrowsmith, Mr., Newport Pagnell
Annesley, Rev. C. F., Banbury, 2 copies
Atterbury, Mr., Milton Keynes
Ayers, Mr. J. D., Newport Pagnell
Ayers, Mrs.,   ditto
Ayers, Mr. J. D., jun., New York

Baker, Mr., Newport Pagnell
Bartlett, Mr., Blandford, Dorset.
Bassett, Mr., Leighton Buzzard
Beard, Rev. J., Rectory, Cranfield
Beaty, Miss, Newport Pagnell, 2 copies
Bedford, Mr.,   ditto
Bell, Mr.,   ditto
Bennell, Mr.,   ditto
Bliss, Mr.,   ditto

c 2

Bliss, Mr., Oundle
Boswell, T. A., Esq., Crawley Grange
Bryant, C. W., Esq., London
Brooks, Rev. J. H., Ridgmount
Brown, Rev. W., Stoke Goldington
Bull, Rev. H., Lathbury
Bull, T., M. D., London
Bull, Rev. T. P., Newport Pagnell
Bull, Rev. J.,   ditto
Bull, Mr. W. B.,   ditto
Bunney, Mr.,   ditto
Burn, Mr.,   ditto
Burn, Mr. W. W. London
Burnett, Mr., Stanton

Capel, J., Esq., London
Cape, Mrs., Great Linford
Capon, Mr. W., London
Carrington, Sir C. E., Chalfont
Carr, Mr. J. R., Newport Pagnell
Cautley, Rev. R., Moulsoe
Cautley, Rev. J., Broughton
Chantler, Mr., Newport Pagnell
Chapman, Mr.,   ditto
Chester, Rev. Anthony, Chicheley Hall
Clarke, Mr., London
Clode, J., Esq., Great Linford
Coales, Mr, D., Newport Pagnell
Coales, Mr. W.,   ditto
Coe, Mr. W ,   ditto
Collingridge, Mr. T., Olney
Collison, Mr. R., Newport Pagnell
Compton, Mr.,   ditto
Cooch, Mr. R. Cromer, Norfolk
Cooch, Mr., Newport Pagnell

Cooper, Mr., Kickles Farm
Cotton, P., Esq., London, 2 copies
Cowley, Mr. G., Winslow
Cowley, J. W., Esq., Buckingham
Cowley, Mrs., Broughton
Cripps, F., Esq., Liverpool, 3 copies
Cripps, Mr., Nottingham, 2 copies

Daniell, Mr., Newport Pagnell
De Wilde, Mr., Northampton
Durden, Mr. H., Blandford, Dorset.
Duncombe, P. D. P., Esq., Brickhill Manor

Elmes, Mr., Newport Pagnell
Edwards, Mr. H.,   ditto
Eames, Mr. J.,   ditto
Egan, Mr. D.,   ditto
Elkins, Mr., Linford, 2 copies
Eve, Mr., Newport Pagnell

Faldo, Mr., Newport Pagnell
French, Mr.,   ditto
Frost, Mr.,   ditto
Fountain, Misses M. A. and C., ditto
Foster, J., Esq., Biggleswade
Fry, Rev. T., Rectory, Emberton
Fulk, C. A. Esq., London

Gawthorn, Mr., Newport Pagnell
Gee, Mr.,   ditto
George, Mr. J.,   ditto
Green, T. A., Esq., Bedford, 2 copies
Groom, Mr., Newport Pagnell
Goodwin, Mr.,   ditto
Gilder, Mr.,   ditto

Hardy, Mrs., Newport Pagnell
Hartley, Mr. Linnell, ditto
Harvey, Mr.,   ditto
Hayllar, Mr.,   ditto
Haynes, Mr.,   ditto
Harris, Mr. J., Bradwell
Hemming, J., Esq., London
Hipwell, Mr., Newport Pagnell
Hives, Mr.,   ditto
Howe, Mr., Milton Keynes
Howe, Mr. W. Jun., Moulsoe
Hull, Mr. T., Newport Pagnell
Humphrey, Mr., Camberwell
Hutton, Mr. F., Wavendon

Kemshead, H., Esq., London
Keep, Mr. J., Birmingham
Keep, Mr., Newport Pagnell
Kidgell, Rev. H., ditto
Kilpin, Miss,   ditto
Kilpin, Mr. W., Bedford
Kipling, Mrs., Newport Pagnell

Law, Rev. W., Great Linford
Leverett, Mr., Newport Pagnell
Levi, Mr.,   ditto
Lilley, Mr. Astwood
Lucas, G., Esq., Newport Pagnell
Lucas, Mr. H.,   ditto
Loyal Chandos Lodge   ditto

Mackinnon, A., Esq., London
Mayor, Mr. J., Northampton
M'William, R., Esq., London
Millar, J., Esq., Newport Pagnell

Morley, Rev. G., Vicarage, Newport Pagnell
Mumford, Mr., London
Morgan, Mr., Tickford Park

Nichols, Mrs., Newport Pagnell
Nash, Mr., Sherington
Nash, Mr. R., North Crawley
Neall, Miss, Newport Pagnell
Neall, Mr. W.,   ditto

Odell, Mr., Cranfield
Odell, Mr. J., Newport Pagnell
Osborn, Mr.,   ditto 2 copies
Oliver, J., Esq., Stony Stratford

Paine, Mrs., Newport Pagnell
Paine, Mr. T.,   ditto 2 copies
Palmer, Mr. J., Olney
Parsons, Mr., Newport Pagnell
Pinfold, C., Esq , Walton, 2 copies
Pike, Mrs. G., Chicheley
Porter, Mr., Newport Pagnell
Powell, Mr. W.,   ditto
Powell, Mr. H.,   ditto
Pratt, Mr., Loughton
Praed, William Tyringham, Esq., M. P., Trevethoe,
     Cornwall, 2 copies
Pretty, Mr., Northampton
Pretyman, Rev. J., Rectory, Sherington, 2 copies
Prust, Rev. J., Northampton

Redden, Mr., Newport Pagnell, 3 copies
Revis, Mr., Olney
Rogers, Mr., Newport Pagnell, 4 copies
Rogers, Mr. G.,   ditto
Rogers, Mr. J.,   ditto

Rose, Rev. F., Rectory, Woughton
Rose, Mr., Bedford
Ross, Mr. G., Wolverton Station

Sheppard, Mr., Newport Pagnell
Shipp, Mr., Blandford, Dorset., 2 copies
Shipp, Mrs. W.,   ditto
Shrieve, Mr., Hanslope
Simcox, Mr, G., Newport Pagnell
Sleath, Mr., Stony Stratford, 2 copies
Smith, Mr. C., Newport Pagnell
Smith, Miss,   ditto
Smith, Mrs., Lathbury
Smith, Mr. S., Buckingham
Staines, Mr. T. E., Newport Pagnell, 3 copies
Staines, Mr. C., Birmingham, 2 copies
Spooner, Mr. E. O., Blandford, Dorset.
Swannell, Mr., Weston Underwood
Sykes, Mr., Newport Pagnell

Talbot, J. H., Esq., Olney, 2 copies
Taylor, Mr., Newport Pagnell
Tomkins, Mrs.,   ditto

Uthwatt, H. Andrewes, Esq., Great Linford

Varney, Mr., Newport Pagnell

Ward, Mrs., Newport Pagnell
Ward, Mr., Chicheley
Warr, Mr., Newport Pagnell
Warren, Mr., Sympson
Warren, Mr. R., Newport Pagnell
Watts, G. W., Esq., London
Watts, W., Esq., Hanslope Park
Webb, Mr., Newport Pagnell

Welton, Mrs., Upper Clapton
Wesley, Mr. T., Newport Pagnell
West, Mr., Lathbury
Wetherell, Rev. R., Rectory, Newton Longueville
Whinfield, Rev. H. W., Filgrave
Whisken, J., Esq., London
Whitworth, Mrs., Newport Pagnell
Wilford, Mr. J.,   ditto
Wilford, Mr. C.,   ditto 2 copies
Wilmer, Mr. J., Gayhurst
Wilkins, Rev. G., Rhendham, Suffolk
Woodley, Mr., Newport Pagnell
Woodroffe, Mr., Olney

Printed by C. TITE, St. John's Street, Newport Pagnell.

Lightning Source UK Ltd.
Milton Keynes UK
UKHW031555300419

341861UK00006B/648/P